Karma and Chaos

New and Collected Essays on Vipassana Meditation

by
Paul R. Fleischman, M.D.

the essay Karma and Chaos *co-authored by*
Forrest D. Fleischman

Vipassana Research Publications • Seattle

VIPASSANA RESEARCH PUBLICATIONS
P.O. BOX 15926
SEATTLE, WASHINGTON, 98115

The two essays, The Therapeutic Action of Vipassana, *and* Why I Sit *were first printed by the Buddhist Publication Society, Sri Lanka, 1986; reprinted 1990, 1995*
ISBN 955-24-0070-8
© *1986 by Paul R. Fleischman*

The two essays, Vipassana Meditation: Healing the Healer, *and* The Experience of Impermanence *were first printed by the Vipassana Research Institute, India,1991; second edition 1995.*
ISBN81-7414-009-3
© *1994 by Paul R. Fleischman*

All photography, both cover art and inside the book, by Forrest D. Fleischman.

First Collected Edition, 1999

ISBN 0-9649484-5-1
© Paul R. Fleischman, 1986, 1994, 1999

Library of Congress Cataloging-in-Publication Data:

Fleischman, Paul R.
     Karma and chaos : new and collected essays on vipassana meditation / by Paul R. Fleischman. — 1st collected ed.
     p. cm.
"The essay Karma and Chaos co-authored by Forrest D. Fleischman".
ISBN 0-9649484-5-1 (paperback)
1. Vipaśynā (Buddhism). 2. Religious life—Buddhism.
3. Buddhism—Doctrines.
I. Fleischman, Forrest D., 1980   II. Title
BQ5630.V5F54 1999
294.3'4435—DC21   99-10912
                         CIP

Printed in Canada

For Rick and Gair

in fond memory of

many long walks

many long talks

Jake's plate

Miss Minnie's cake

and a love of truth in language.

Contents

Preface

November 8, 1998, I am conducting a meditation course in the lineage of my teacher, at the Northwest Vipassana Center. Although forty people are in the meditation hall, it is so quiet that I can hear every tap of the syncopated rain drops falling from the Pacific clouds. These Vipassana students seem noble to me, each one earnest in his or her calm and rectitude. They are a varied lot, freely admitted to the course, farmers, doctors, students, mothers, and outdoorsmen. As I sit in front with open eyes, I observe their stillness in ranks, and recognize them not just as the individuals they are, but as the cresting wave on a river of bodies, that flows through time, from era to era. Each individual arises, stays for some time, then passes away, and behind them come others—a continuous flood of silent meditators rippling up and flowing through the world, century after century, weaving into the landmass of humanity a freshet of harmony, compassion, love and equanimity. Without moving, they flow forward, emerging from invisible beginnings, motionlessly surging toward me. I, too, wish to be entering the stream.

II

This book is intended to inspire people on the path of Vipassana meditation. It is itself the product of the Vipassana-derived energy and enthusiasm of Mr. Richard Crutcher, who was determined to make these essays more easily available to readers in the Western hemisphere.

Four of the essays in this volume have circulated among meditators for many years in editions and reprints published in India and Sri Lanka. These articles have sparked continuous, warm feedback from readers of all backgrounds from around the world, who have described the clarification, recommitment, or inspiration that they derived from the writing. Demand for these essays has never abated. Unfortunately they remained known only to an "in-group." Noticing their catalytic effect, Vipassana Research Publications committed itself to the task of bringing both the original four articles and more like them to a wider readership in the West. I was admonished to overcome doubt, to write more, with the particular focus of addressing concerns of the new legions of Vipassana students, who are apt to be lay men and women, meditating amidst domestic and professional contexts, and who hail from scientific, nontraditional worldviews.

"Why I Sit" describes my original dubious motives and misperceptions about meditation, and has provided a welcome door for people who are comforted to find that the path doesn't begin in wisdom, but in a concoction of human foibles and aspirations. One Vipassana student told me: "I was glad to find someone so willing to say such embarrassing things on paper without censorship." The path itself has changed me since I wrote this essay in 1982, but it remains a valuable reminder that it is pied people who keep the wheel of Vipassana turning.

The next three essays in this book, spanning a period of thought approximately fifteen years long, are about the interface between psychiatry, psychotherapy and Vipassana. The psychological healing professions—psychiatry, psychology, social work, nursing, counselling, etc.—are probably the commonest source of livelihood for Vipassana meditators in the USA and Canada. These articles address such issues as how Vipassana heals, its relationship to the personal life of professionals, its common grounds, limits, and differences from the psychotherapeutic endeavors. I hope the writing will inspire even more therapists to practice Vipassana, and will keep both professionalism and meditation communicating, yet distinct and pure. While there are ways in which they fertilely overlap, they also occupy vastly divergent realms.

The next two essays ("The Experience of Impermanence" and "Touchdown *Anicca*") deal with the focal realization which Vipassana facilitates. They describe the experience available through meditation, and its relevance and application to modern life. Meditation is not just a practice for bark-encrusted hermits. The world beyond self can be known directly and enhances every situation, from a Seattle office to a Massachusetts kitchen, from marriage to death.

The final essay, "Karma and Chaos," coauthored by Forrest D. Fleischman, is the longest, maybe the toughest going and the closest to the author's heart. While not everyone needs so much cogitation to grow with Vipassana, it nevertheless addresses issues that have been vital to me in my development on the path and I suspect may be as well for many other scientifically educated 20th and 21st century Vipassana practitioners. I, too, am a product of scientific, intellectual skepticism and can't give allegiance to anything that I can't make sense of. The ethical ec-stasis that lies at the heart of Vipassana insight, and its implications for a coherent world-view, have impelled and challenged my personal progress. Vipassana not only changes us profoundly, it also changes the way we understand and relate to reality, making us simultaneously more rational and more receptive to a deeper, more numinous vision of the dimensions of causality and connection. This particular vision would not have jelled without my coauthor's concepts and clarity.

III

The series of essays in this book move with time. When I wrote "Why I Sit," I was the parent of a toddler. About fifteen years later, the two of us, both meditators, coauthored "Karma and Chaos."

I have written these essays as a donation, with particular gratitude to my friends who have hammered, roofed, plumbed and cooked at Vipassana centers where I have sat but never built. The writing is royalty-free, with my share donated towards public education about Vipassana.

Many people have helped me on the path, and I have acknowledged them in print elsewhere. I am sure they can also feel their solicitude, humor, or friendship emanating back from these pages. In particular, I would like to acknowledge the help of my Vipassana *Ācariya*, S.N. Goenka, whose role in my life is beyond praise; Rick Crutcher, publisher, editor and sustaining friend; Bhikkhu Bodhi for first publishing two of these essays in the Buddhist Publication Society Wheel Series; Susan K. Fleischman, cherished and revered partner in Dhamma; and Forrest D. Fleischman, my coconspirator in conceptual models, skepticism, and wonder. We have travelled together down many rivers. The home to which Odysseus returned was changed forever. To be at home in the homeless, we need a map and compass, confidence in our capacities, trust in our companions, and a love of wide river banks and open sky. Every campsite is left behind in the morning.

Dhamma Kuñja, the Grove of Truth
November 1998

Prologue

Sacred Partnership

There is a sacred partnership between reason and faith. The student of the path progresses by joining intelligence, logic and investigation to hope, perseverance and reverence. Science and meditation both give light, like the moon and the sun.

There is a sacred partnership between mundane and transcendent. Only by validating and engaging the suffering world can its limits be glimpsed.

There is a sacred partnership between the individual and the path. Only by joining its history, its people and its process can a person dip into the experience to which the path leads. The path proceeds through relationships.

There is a sacred partnership among those who build a home dedicated to truth and harmony. They emerge into the same circle of daylight, having journeyed across time on the wings of shared development. Now they meditate together. Their home is a safe harbor for others; a ship's prow skillfully traversing the ocean; a lamp in the darkness.

Why I Sit

This morning the first thing I did was to sit for an hour. I have done that religiously for many years, and have spent many evenings, days and weeks doing the same. The English word "meditate" until recently had a vague meaning, referring to any one of a set of activities like extended deep thought, or prayer, or religious contemplation. Recently, "meditation" gained a pseudo-specificity: "T.M.," deep relaxation, or alpha-wave conditioning, with connotations of Hinduized cult phenomena like mantras, gurus, and altered states of consciousness. To "sit" is a basic word, with connotations ranging from chicken-coops to boredom and sagacity, so it forms a neutral starting point for an explanation of why I have spent thousands upon thousands of hours "sitting," and why I have made this activity the center of my life.

I

I would like to know myself. It is remarkable that while ordinarily we spend most of our lives studying, contemplating, observing, and manipulating the world around us, the structured gaze of the thoughtful mind is so rarely turned inwards. This avoidance must measure some anxiety, reluctance, or fear. That makes me still more curious. Most of our lives are spent in externally oriented functions that distract from self-observation. This relentless, obsessive drive persists independently of survival needs such as food and warmth, and even of pleasure. Moment for moment, we couple ourselves to sights, tastes, words, motions, or electric stimuli, until we fall dead. It is striking how many ordinary activities, from smoking a pipe to watching sunsets, veer towards, but ultimately avoid, sustained attention to the reality of our own life.

So it is not an intellectual intrigue with the platonic dictum that leads me to sit, but an experience of myself and my fellow human as stimulus-bound, fundamentally out of control, alive only in reaction. I want to know, to simply observe, this living person as he is, not just as he appears while careening from event to event. Of course, this will undoubtedly be helpful to me as a psychiatrist, but my motives are more fundamental, personal, and existential.

I am interested in my mind, and in my body. Previous to my having cultivated the habit of sitting, I had thought about myself, and had used my body as a tool in the world, to grip a pen or to chop firewood, but I had never systematically, rigorously, observed my body—what it feels like, not just with a shy, fleeting glance, but moment after moment for hours and days at a time; nor had I committed myself to observe the reciprocal influence of mind and body in states of exhaustion and rest, hunger, pain, relaxation, arousal, lethargy, or concentration. My quest for knowing is not merely objective and scientific. This mind-and-body is the vessel of my life. I want to drink its nectar, and if necessary, its sludge, but I want to know it with the same organic immersion that sets a snow goose flying ten thousand miles every Winter and Spring.

It seems to me that the forces of creation, the laws of nature, out of which this mind and body arose, must be operative in me, now, continuously, and whenever I make an effort to observe them. The activity of creation must be the original and continuing cause of my life. I would like to know these laws, these forces, my maker, and observe, even participate, in the ongoing creation.

Newton founded modern science with his assumption that there is one continuous world, one unbroken order, one set of laws governing both earth and sky; so along with this great tradition, and along with the ancient religions of

India as well, I assume that the physics of the stars is the physics of my body also. The laws of chemistry and biology, predicated on the laws of physics, are also uniform throughout nature. Since these laws operate continuously, without reserve or sanctuary, but uniformly and pervasively, I deduce that eternal, unbroken laws operate in me, created me, and create me, that my life is an expression of them continuously linked by cause and effect to all that antedated, all that follows, and all that is co-existent; and that, to the extent that I am conscious and capable of learning, a systematic study and awareness of creation's ways is available to me if I live with attention to this field.

Even if I am frequently incapable of actually observing the most basic levels of reality, at least the mental and physical phenomena that bombard me are predicated on nature's laws, and must be my laboratory to study them. I want to sing like a bird, like a human. I want to grow and rot like a tree, like a man. I want to sit with my mind and body as they cast up and swirl before me and inside me the human stuff which is made of and ordered by the matter and laws governing galaxies and wrens.

Because the harmony in me is at once so awesome and sweet and overwhelming that I love its taste yet can barely compel myself to glimpse it, I want to sit with the great determination that I need to brush aside the fuzz of distraction, the lint of petty concerns. To sit is to know myself as an unfolding manifestation of the universals of life. A gripping, unending project. Hopefully one I can pursue even when I look into death's funnel. For me, this knowing is a great force, and a great pleasure.

II

I sit because of, for, and with, an appreciation of daily life. The great poets sing of the omnipresent ordinary, pregnant with revelation—but I know how easily and recurrently my own life yields to distraction, irritation, tunnel vision. I do not want to miss my life the way I once missed a plane at La

Guardia airport. It may be ironic that simply to wiggle free of daydreams and worries I need a technique, a practice, a discipline, but I do; and I bow to that irony by doing what I *must* do to pry my mind off ephemeral worries, to wake to more dawns, to *see* my child unravel through his eddying transformations.

It may be contrary that I must work so hard to be at peace with myself, but I do; and I have become increasingly convinced, learning as I sit and live and sit and live, that "being at peace" is not a state of mind, but a state of mind and body. At the core of my life is a receptive drinking in. The simple beauty of things keeps flooding in to me. I live for this draught, and build my life around it. Yet it slips away. I can try to crash back through by taking dramatic journeys—to India, or to lakes at tree-line in the Rocky Mountains—but this kind of breath-taking beauty is only an interlude, a punctuation mark. It reminds me of what I intended to emphasize in my life, but like an exclamation point, it has limited use.

The clear direct sentence—the death sentence, the sentence of love—ends with a mere period. This declarative beauty is more like looking up over the slums of Montreal to see the moon wearing a pendant of Venus in 4:00 a.m. darkness. I am describing not what is sought or built, but what I discover when the walls fall away. Similarly when I walk alone in the autumn forest, up and down gneiss and schist hills and ridges of Vermont, and I become confused whether that intense pulsating drumming is the "booming" of grouse wings, or my own heart, strained by the last climb. This is an experience that is a metphor also. We sometimes feel our body, our life, beating in recognition. We absorb a dimension of reality that is the same inside and outside, an inner, lawful pulse to things. The tuning fork of my life hums in response to the living world.

This receipt—like a parent accepting back a soggy, half-eaten cracker—requires, for me, a framework, a matrix in my body, that simple as it should be, I do not simply have. This knowing requires a bodily preparation. I sit to open my pores, skin and mind both, to the life that surrounds me, inside and outside, at least more often if not all the time, as it arrives at my doorstep. I sit to exercise the appreciative, receptive, peaceful mode of being filled up by the ordinary and inevitable. For example, the sagging floorboards in the crooked bedroom where I am a husband. Or my two-year-old son, tugging one splinter at a time, to help me stack firewood in new January snow.

III

I feel a need for a rudder, a keel, a technique, a method a way to continue on course. I need ceaselessly increasing moments of self-control (though not constriction, deadening, or inhibition). It seems to me that the best of human life is lived on a narrow ledge, like a bridge over a stream in Nepal, or like a trail in the Grand Canyon, between two chasms. On the one side is desire, on the other side is fear. Possibly it is because of my work as a psychiatrist, often with essentially normal people, who are nonetheless pushed and pulled about by their inner forces like tops, that I feel so sensitized to these faults that can send seismic shudders through apparently solid lives. But my own life has ground enough for these observations.

Sitting is, among other things, the practice of self-control. While sitting one does not get up, or move, or make that dollar, or pass that test, or receive reassurance from that phone call. But military training, or violin lessons, or medical school, are also routes to self-control in this ordering and restrictive sense. Sitting is self-control around specific values. Observation replaces all action. What is the point of committing one's life to this practice, only to spend the time with erotic daydreams, or anxious yearnings for promotion and recognition? Of course, those will happen anyway. They are part of the human make-up. Cultures would not have proliferated the ubiquitous moral codes, the

Ten Commandments, if we were not so replete with ten million urges.

But moral invective, preaching, always seemed feeble to me—possibly just a measure of my wild horses and snails. I need a constantly usable, constantly renewable lens to see through my yearnings into my loves, to see through my anxieties into my faith. What is a bedrock feeling, the core of my identity, and what is a titillation that will ultimately be discarded? What characters walk in front of the mirror of my soul day after day, year after year, and who are the clowns that steal the stage for a scene?

An hour of sitting is one thing: longer periods another. Once a year, under the guidance of a teacher, I sit for ten days, all day. That kind of practice induces pain. To face pain has become a regular, inescapable part of my life. It is for most people—laborers, poor, infirm, cold, infected, hungry people throughout the world. But I have not elected sentimental, identificatory masochism. I am looking at another side of myself. While I spontaneously seek to avoid pain, a higher wisdom than knee-jerk reaction tells me that, in Socrates' words: "...pain and pleasure are never present to a man at the same instant, and yet he who pursues either is compelled to take the other; their bodies are two, but they are joined by a single head." (Phaedo)

Just how serious am I about being who I said I was? How integrated do I want to be with this screaming body that has to be fed, slept, positioned just right, or it howls unbearably? I sit because I know I need a self-control that does not lecture or stomp on my tendencies, but reorganizes desire into love, and pain and fear into faith.

IV

As I understand it, love is not an emotion, but an organization of emotions. It is not a room, but a dwelling; not a bird, but a migratory flyway. It is a structure of emotions, a meta-emotion. This is in contrast to love understood as a sentimental gush of attachment, or as romantic sexuality.

Sitting has helped me to find love, to live by love, or at least, to live more by love. It has helped me come alive as a husband, father, psychiatrist, and citizen, within the bounds of my character and capabilities. It has pried me open beyond either my previous sentimental position or my rational moral knowledge and has given me a tool, a practice, an activity expressive of love. For me it is both crowbar and glue.

As Erik Erikson has written, it is only "ambivalence that makes love meaningful—or possible." In other words, it is only because we are both separate, and united, that love exists. If we had no individual existence, no personal drives, there would be merely the homogeneous glob of the world, devoid of emotion, unknowing, like a finger on a hand. Yet if we were irreconcilably separate there would only be self-maintaining cold stars co-existing in dead space. I understand love to mean the organization of human emotions into those complex states where separation and merging, individuality and immersion, self and selflessness paradoxically co-exist. Only an individual can love; and only one who has ceased to be one can love. Sitting has helped me develop both these poles. It breaks me open where I get stuck; and where I fall off as a chip, it sticks me back on to the main piece.

Sitting pushes me to the limit of my self-directed effort; it mobilizes my willed, committed direction, yet it also shatters my self-protective, self-defining maneuvers, and my simple self-definition. It both builds and dismantles "me". Every memory, every hope, every yearning, every fear floods in. I no longer can pretend to be one selected set of my memories or traits.

If observed, but not reacted upon, all these psychic contents become acceptable, obviously part of myself (for there they are in my own mind, right in front of me); yet also impersonal, causally-linked, objective phenomena-in-the-world that move ceaselessly, relentlessly, across the screen of my existence, without my effort, without my control, without *me*. I can see more, tolerate more, in my inner life,

at the same time that I am less driven by these forces. Like
storms and doves, they are the personae of nature, crossing
one inner sky. Psychic complexity swirls up from the dust
of cosmetic self-definition. At the same time, the determination and endurance I have to muster to just observe, grow
like muscles with exercise. Naturally the repetition of this
mixture of tolerance and firmness extrapolates beyond its
source in sitting, out to relationships.

There is little I have heard from others—and it is my
daily business to hear—that I have not seen in myself as I
sit. But I also know the necessity of work, training and re-
straint. Dependence, loneliness, sensuality, exhaustion,
hunger, petulance, perversion, miserliness, yearning, inflation are my old friends. I can greet them openly and warmly
in people close to me, both because I know them from the
inside and therefore cannot condemn them without con-
demning myself; and also because I have been learning to
harness and ride their energy. To love, I try to hold the complex reality of myself at the same time that I try to catch the
complex reality of another.

I have known my wife for decades. We have dated and
swam, married and fought, traveled, built cabins, bought
houses, delivered and diapered together; in short, we have
attained the ordinary and ubiquitous. In a world of three
billion people, this achievement ranks with literacy, and
would have no bearing on why I sit, except that it does.
Even the inevitable is fragile. I, we, am, and are, buffered by
un-shy thanks. We are sharpened by life with an edge.

I sit and life moves through me, my married life too.
This sphere also takes its turn before my solitary, impeach-
able witness to my own existence and its eternal
entanglements. As a married man, I sit as if in a harbor from
my selfish pettiness, where the winds of my annoyance or
anger have time to pass; I sit as a recipient of a generous
outpouring of warmth that I have time to savor; I sit as a
squash or pumpkin with his own slightly fibrous and only

moderately sweet but nonetheless ample life to lay on some-one else's table; I sit as one oxen in a team pulling a cart filled with rocking horses, cars, and porches that need paint; I sit knowing myself as a sick old man of the future awaiting the one person who can really attend, or as the future one whose voice alone can wave death back behind someone else's hospital curtain for another hour; I sit as a common man of common desire, and as a dreamer who with the bricks of shared fate is building a common dream; and I sit alone in my own life anyway.

How fortunate to have this cave, this sanctuary, this frying-pan, this rock, and this mirror of sitting, in which to forge, drop, haul, touch, release my love and not get lost. To sit is the compass by which I navigate the seas of married love. It is also the string by which I trip up the fox on his way to the chicken coop. To live is a deep yearning and hard work. It cannot be done alone! There are many ways to re-ceive help, and many ways to give it. Martin Buber says that men and women cannot love without a third point to form a stable triangle: a god, task, calling, or meaning beyond their dyadic individuality. What about two who just know the pole star?

There is a joke in "Peanuts": "I love mankind. It's just people that I hate." I think love is concrete and abstract. If it is only an amorphous generalized feeling, it remains a plati-tude, a wish, a defense against real entanglement. This is what sounds hollow in the pious, sanctimonious "Love" of some churches and martyrs. But if love is only concrete, immediate, personal, it remains in the realm of possession, privatism, materialism, narcissism. This is the paternalistic love a person has for his house, cars, family. My understand-ing is that actual love expands outward in both spheres. Riding the wings of the ideal, it sweeps up and carries along those who are encountered.

I sit to better love my wife, and those friends and com-panions with whom I share even a day's journey on my flight from the unknown to the unknown. It is difficult to love the one with whom my fate is most closely entangled during those moments when I would like to batter down the corridors of that fate. But it is easy to love her when we sweeten each other's tea. It is easy to feel affection for friends I encounter on weekends devoted to family life and outdoor play; it is difficult to let our lives, our health and finances entangle. Such an embrace threatens private safety. And it is more difficult still to try to place this way of being, first among all others, and risk myself over and over again.

Shall I keep all my money, or risk it on a charitable principle? Shall I study the text sanctioned by the authorities, or sing out from my heart? When I sit, money does me little good; approval evaporates; but the tone of the strings of my heart, for better or worse, is inescapable. I sit to tie myself to the mast, to hear more of the song of elusive and unavoidable love.

V

A baby looks fragile, but if you neglect his meal or hold him the wrong way, your eardrums will have to reckon with an awesome wrath! Anger springs from and participates in the primary survival instinct of the organism. Yet how much trouble it causes us in daily life, not to mention large-scale social relations! Probably the height of inanity would be to sit, angry. What is the point of such impotent stewing? I sit to grow up, to be a better person, to see trivial angers rise up and pass away, arguments on which I put great weight on Thursday morning fade by Thursday noon; and to be compelled to reorder, restructure, rethink my life, so that, living well, my petty anger is orchestrated ahead of time into flexibility, co-operation, or the capacity to see other viewpoints. Sitting helps me to transcend the irritable, petulant infant in me.

But that only solves the periphery of the problem. I am no longer angry about my diapers. I am angry that my votes and taxes have been turned to oppressing other nations; I am angry that I will be judged for the rest of my life by multiple choice exams; I am angry that research is ignored and dogma is used to coerce one religion's point of view; I am angry that mountains are scoured for energy to manufacture throw-away soda cans. I sit also, then, to express my anger, and the form of expression is determination. I sit with force, will, and, when the pain mounts, something that feels fierce. Sitting helps me harness authentic anger.

I have been sitting at least fifteen hours a week for years, and when, as often happens, I am asked how I find the time, I know that part of the certainty in my aim is an anger that will not allow the rolling woodlands and hilltop pastures of my psyche to be bulldozed by TV, non-nutritional food, fabricated news, tweed socialization, pedantic file-cabinets of knowledge, or loyalty rallies to leaders, states, gods, and licensures. The voices of the herd will not so easily drive me from my forest cabin of deeply considered autonomy and honest talk, because I have had practice in this sort of firmness. A child's anger is the kindling of adult will. I can stay true to myself yet mature, be willed but not willful, by sitting in the spirit of Woody Guthrie's song: "Don't you push me, push me, push me, don't you push me down!"

VI

As I understand it, the lifelong disciplined practice of sitting is not exactly religion, but is not *not* a religion either. For myself, I am not bound to scriptures, dogma, hierarchies; I have taken no proscriptions on my intelligence, or on my political autonomy; nor have I hidden from unpleasant realities by concretizing myth. But I have become increasingly aware of the inextricable role of faith in my practice.

The faith I have been discovering in myself is not blind, irrational, unsubstantiated, or wishful ideas. Following the definitive clarification of these English terms by Paul Tillich, I would call those former "beliefs." I hope sitting has helped me to free myself from my beliefs even further than my scientific education did. Nor does faith mean what I live for—goals, personal preferences, commitments, and loves. These are ideals, visions, tastes—very important—but not faith. Faith is what I *live by,* what empowers my life. The battery, the heart-pump, of my becoming. It is not the other shore, but the boat. It is not what I know, but how I know. It is present, rather than past or future, and is my most authentic, total reaction, a gut reaction deeper than my guts. Tillich defined faith as a person's ultimate concern—the bedrock of what we in fact take seriously. I would like to describe faith, as I have found it, to be the hunger of my existence.

Hunger springs up from my body. It antedates my mental and psychological life, and can even run havoc over them. I do not eat because of what I believe or hope or wish for, or because of what an authority prescribes or what I read. I eat because I am hungry. My body is a dynamic, metabolizing system, an energy exchanger, constantly incorporating, reworking, remolding—this is the vitality intrinsic to the life of any oak, deer or human. This creature I am consumes, reworks, then creates more emotional, spiritual life. Not what I digest, but the ordered process in me that gives coherence and direction to this continuous organism, constitutes faith.

Faith is not something I have (e.g. "I believe!"); it is something that I realize has already been given to me, on which the sense of "me" is predicated. I find it or receive it, not once, but intermittently and continuously. It is not a set of thoughts, and it provides no concrete, reducible answers. Who am I? What is this life? Where does it come from? Where is it headed? I don't know. On these important questions, I have no beliefs. Yet no day has shaken this strange bird from his perch!

I sit with impassioned neutrality. Why? This activity is not *in order to get* answers with which to live my life. It *is* my life. Bones are not in order to hang skin and muscle on. (In scientific thought, too, teleology—goal-directed thinking—leads nowhere. Who knows the goal of the universe? Then what is the goal of any part of it?) I eat, I read, I work, I play, I sit. If I have no big intellectual belief by which I can justify my day, myself, my life, my suppertime, I eat anyway! Usually with pleasure.

I am neither an existentialist, a Marxist, nor an anorectic. Hunger is a spontaneous action of life in me. The hunger of my existence also demands sustenance daily. The nourishment I take becomes my body; the sustenance I take becomes the unfolding process of "me". To be alive, to be alert, to be observant, to be at peace with myself and all others—vibrating in ceaseless change—unmoving: I find this is my sustaining passage through the incandescent world doing the same.

As a scientific fact, I know I am alive only inside the body of life. Physically, I am aware of myself as a product of other lives—parents, ancestors. I breathe the oxygen created by plants, so that, as I breathe in and out, I am a tube connected to the whole life of the biosphere, a tiny, dependent digit. Through digestion and metabolism I biotransform the organic molecules created by plants and animals, which I call food, into other biochemicals with which I mold this form called my body, which is constantly, continuously being remolded, reformed, like a cloud. And this form will eventually cease its regeneration and vanish, as it arose, from causes, forces in nature.

It is easy for me to comprehend this description of physical reality, which is so obvious and scientific. But my person, my psychological reality, is also a product of causes: things I have been taught, experiences I have had, cultural beliefs, social forces. This uninterrupted web of causality—physical, biological, psychological, cultural—connecting from past to future, and out across contemporaneousness, is the ocean in which the bubble of my life briefly floats.

Death must be inevitable for such an ephemeral bubble. Yet while it is here, I can feel how vital is this breathing, pulsating being, alive, resonant in exchange with past and future, people and things—transducer and knower.

The faith that underlies my practice is not in my mind, but is the psychological correlate of animation. I experience faith not as a thought, but as the overwhelming mood which drives this thrust upward of emerging. By sitting I can know, assume, become, this direct hum of energy. Retrospectively, verbally, I call this "faith." When I am bored, pained, lazy, distracted, worried, I find myself sitting anyway, not because I believe it is good, or will get me into heaven, nor because I have particular will power. My life is expressing its trajectory. All mass is energy, Einstein showed. My life is glowing, and I sit in the light.

VII

Sitting enabled me to see, and compelled me to acknowledge, the role that death had already played, and still continues to play, in my life. Every living creature knows that the sum total of its pulsations is limited. As a child I wondered: Where was I before I was born? Where will I be after I die? How long is forever and when does it end? The high school student of history knew that every hero died; I saw the colors of empires wash back and forth over the maps in the books like tides. (Not me!) Where can I turn that impermanence is not the law? I try to hide from this as well as I can, behind my youth (already wrinkling, first around the eyes, and graying), and health insurance: but no hideout works.

Every day ends with darkness; things must get done today or they will not happen at all. And, funny, rather than sapping my appetite, producing "nausea" (which may be due to rich French sauces rather than real philosophy), the pressure of nightfall helps me to treasure life. Isn't this the most universal human observation and counsel? I aim each swing of the maul more accurately at the cracks in the oak cordwood I am splitting. I choose each book I read with precision and reason. I hear the call to care for and love my child and the forest trails that I maintain as a pure ringing note of mandate. I sit at the dawn of day and day passes. Another dawn, but the series is limited, so I swear in my inner chamber I will not miss a day.

Sitting rivets me on the psychological fact that death is life's door. No power can save me. Because I am aware of death, and afraid, I lean my shoulder into living not automatically and reactively, like an animal, nor passively and pleadingly, like a child pretending he has a father watching over him, but with conscious choice and decision of what will constitute each fleeting moment of my life. I know that my petals cup a volatile radiance. But to keep this in mind in turn requires that an ordinary escapist constantly reencounters the limit, the metronome of appreciation, death.

I sit because knowing I will die enriches, and excoriates my life, so I have to go out of my way to seek discipline and the stability that is necessary for me to really face it. To embrace life I must shake hands with death. For this, I need practice. Each act of sitting is a dying to outward activity, a relinquishment of distraction, a cessation of anticipatory gratification. It is life now, as it is. Some day this austere focus will come in very, very handy. It already has.

VIII

I sit to be myself, independent of my own or others' judgments. Many years of my life were spent being rated, primarily in school, but, as an extension of that, among friends and in social life. As much as I tried to fight off this form of addiction, I got hooked anyway. As often happens, out of their concern for me, my parents combed and brushed me with the rules of comparison: I was good at this, or not good, or as good, or better, or worse, or the best, or no good at all.

Today I find that sitting reveals the absurdity of comparative achievement. My life consists of what I actually live, not the evaluations that float above it. Sitting enables me to slip beyond that second, commenting, editor's mind, and to burrow in deep towards immediate reality. I have made progress in becoming a mole, an empty knapsack, a boy on a day when school is cancelled. What is there to gain or lose as I sit? Who can I beat, who can I scramble after? Just this one concrete day, all this, and only this, comes to me on the tray of morning, flashes out now.

I am relieved to be more at home in myself, with myself. I complain less. I can lose discussions, hopes, or self-expectations, more easily and much less often, because the talking, hoping, and doing is victory enough already. Without props or toys or comfort, without control of the environment, I have sat and observed who I am when there was no one and nothing to give me clues. It has happened that I have sat, asked for nothing, needed nothing, and felt full. Now my spine and hands have a different turgor. When I am thrown off balance, I can fall somewhat more like a cat than like a two-by-four. When I sit, no one—beloved or enemy—can give me what I lack, or take away what I am.

So as I live all day, I can orient myself into becoming the person I will have to live with when I next sit. No one else's commentary of praise or blame can mediate my own confrontation with the observed facts of who I am. I'm not as bad as I thought I was—and worse. But I'm definitely sprouting and real. It's a pleasure to relinquish yearning and fighting back, and to permit ripples. And I sit to share companionship with other spring bulbs. I feel like one leaf in a deciduous forest: specific, small, fragile, all alone with my fate, yet shaking in a vast and murmuring company.

IX

Sitting is a response to, and an expression of, my social and historical conditions. Although I practice an ancient way that has been passed on from person to person for two and a half millennia and must be useful and meaningful under a variety of conditions, I sought and learned this practice for reasons particular to myself.

One of the most powerful forces that pushed my life into the form it has taken was World War II, which ended, almost to the day, when I was born. It was a backdrop, very present in my parents' sense of the world, and in other adults around me, that left little scope for hope. Fear seemed the only rational state of mind, self-defense the only rational posture. Cultured, civilized men had just engaged in an extended, calculated, concerted sadism the scope of which is incomprehensible. Victory by goodness had brought reactive evil: nuclear weapons. The world-view I was taught and absorbed was to study hard, save my money, and build my own self-protective world, using the liberal, rational, scientific cultures as stepping stones to an anxious fiefdom of private family life. It was only in that private space that the sweet kernel of affection and idealistic aspiration could be unveiled. I did that well, and to some extent it worked.

Yet at the same time I had been guided to, and later chose to, spend my summers in the woods learning about white-tailed deer, mosquitoes, freedom, and canoes, surrounded, it seemed, by a primal monistic goodness that I located in nature and those who lived close to it. I read Thoreau the way many people read the Bible. The world of cold streams running under shady hemlocks, and its ecstatic prophets, seemed an antidote to the haunted, dull, convention-bound, anxious lives of my immediate environment. Moving between these two worlds, I learned a dialogue of terror and ecstasy, survivorship and care, that filled me with an urgency to find the middle way. This motivated a search that led through intense intellectual exploration in college, medical school, and psychiatric training, and finally to the art of "sitting," as taught by S.N. Goenka, a Vipassana meditation teacher from whom my wife and I first took a course near New Delhi in 1974. Those ten days of nothing but focusing on the moment by moment reality of body and mind, with awareness and equanimity, gave me the opportunity ironically both to be more absolutely alone and isolated than I had every been before, and at the same time to cast my lot with a tradition, a way, as upheld, manifested, explained, and transmitted by a living person. I am continuously grateful to Goenka for the receipt of this technique.

Vipassana meditation was preserved in Asia for two thousand five hundred years since its discovery by Gotama, the historical Buddha. His technique of living was labeled, by western scholars, "Buddhism," but it is not an "ism," a system of thought. It is a practice, a method, a tool of living persons. It does not end its practitioner's search. For me, it provides a compass, a spy glass, a map for further journeys. With daily practice, and intensive retreats mixed into the years, I find the marriage of autonomy and heritage, membership and lonely continuity. Vipassana is the binoculars—now I can search for the elusive bird.

Before I received instructions in how to sit, my journey through life was predominantly intellectual. I had found lectures and books to be inspiring, suggestive, artful, but evasive. One could advise, one could talk, one could write. But sitting is a way for me to stand for something, to sit as something, not just with words, but with my mind, body, and life. Here is a way to descend by stages, protected by teacher, teaching, technique, and practice, into the light and darkness in me, the Hitler and Buddha in me, the frightened child of a holocaust world riding a slow bus in winter through dark city streets, and the striding, backpacking youth wandering through sunlight cathedrals of Douglas fir, who, shouting or whimpering, spans the vocabulary of human potentials from sadism to love.

I now can see that I carry the whip and boots of the torturer, I suffer with the naked, I drink from mountain streams with poets and explorers. All these lives live in me. And I find ways, often covert and symbolic, to express these psychological potentials in me as overt actions in my daily life. Everything I am springs from the universally human. I cause myself, I express myself, as the conditions of the world roll through me. I see this fact, as I sit, as clearly as I see the impact of history and the inspiration of vision. I sit in clear confrontation with everything that has impinged on me and caused me to react, and in reacting, I mold myself.

Life begins in a welter of conditions; mere reactions to these conditions forge limitations; awareness of and conscious response to conditions produces freedom. This clarity regarding my choices enables me to return from sitting to action as a more focused, concentrated vector of knowing, empathic life.

Sitting itself transforms my motives for sitting. I started in my own historical circumstances, but I was given a technique that has been useful in millions of circumstances over thousands of years. I started with personal issues, and I have been given timeless perspectives to broaden my viewpoint. My search is particular, but not unique. The transmission of this tool has made my work possible. Because others have launched the quest for a fully human life, because others will follow, my own frailty, or villainy, can become meaningful, because these are the soil which I must use to grow. And my own efforts, however great they feel to me, are in the shadow of the much greater efforts of others.

I can flower as one shrub in a limitless forest of unending cycles of life. To flower, for a human being, is to work on the science of honest observation that enables a true picture of humanity to be born. Even coming from my conditioning of nihilism and dread, without the comfort of simple beliefs, aware of awesome human evil and hatred, of wars that kill decamillions, I can be, I will be, an expression of contentless faith. I cannot be much but I can root deep into what is true, how to see it, and how to pass it on.

In response to the overwhelming sense of evil, fear, meaninglessness, and paranoid privatism of my times, and in response to the hope, idealism, and pregnant sense of eternity of my youth, I learned to sit, to better stand for what I found most true. This helps me live out what had before been an unconscious faith. It helps me express something healing, useful (in both my personal and professional life), and meaningful to me despite apparently absurd conditions, because it is a link to the universal. It puts me in touch with the fundamentally human that is present in every gesture of mine, and every action of other people, in each immediacy. This in turn has enabled me to join with the generative dance of nature. I practice knowing myself, and make that the workshop of the day. I refrain from measuring events by my own inchworm life. I frequently forget time, and so join history.

X

I sit in solitude to lose my isolation. What is least noble in me rises up to the surface of my mind, and this drives me on to be more than I was. When I am most shut into my dark self I find the real source of my belonging.

Freud claimed that the bedrock of human fear is castration anxiety. This, he felt, is more feared than death itself. I understand castration anxiety to mean physical pain, bodily mutilation, and social isolation, ostracism, loss of membership, generativity, continuity in the cycle of generations. The two greatest difficulties I have, in fact, faced while sitting for extended hours or days are physical pain, and the loss of the social position that I had previously seemed headed for and entitled to in the community of men. Pain that starts in the knees or back can flood the whole body and burn on and on. The self-protection of calculated membership, and its comfortable rewards, are lost to me in those aching, endless hours.

I imagine my others options: a better house, winter vacations in the tropics, the respect of colleagues listening to me speak as I climb the career ladder. I imagine the financial crises I am less prepared to withstand. I imagine the

humiliating rejection that crushes the refugee from poverty
or racism or any form of powerlessness, all of which are in
my heritage and possibly in my future (and in anyone's heritage or future if you look far enough). Why do I sit there?
A thrush hops onto a low limb at the edge of a wooded
clearing and shatters the Vermont evening with triumphant
song. Knowing yet staying, I am an inheritor and transmit-
ter, flooded with gifts from those who loved and left their
trace; and this still, glowing, posture is the song of my species.

Sitting helps me overcome my deepest fears. I become
freer to live from my heart, and to face the consequences,
but also to reap the rewards of this authenticity. Much of
what I called pain was really loneliness and fear. It passes,
dissolves, with that observation. The vibrations of my body
are humming the song that can be heard only when dawn
and dusk are simultaneous, instantaneous, continuous. I feel
a burst of stern effort is a small price to pay to hear this
inner music—fertile music from the heart of life itself.

It has been my fortune along the way to find and follow many friends who, like long unobserved mushrooms,
no longer can be shaken from the stump because their roots
have reached the heartwood. From them I have caught a
glimmer of two lights: devotion and integrity. And it has
been an extra pleasure—and sometimes I think a necessity—
to be able to sit beside my wife. Even the stars move in
constellations.

XI

I sit to find mental freedom. I was lucky to be able to think
rationally, logically, scientifically, in a culture where focused,
aggressive thought is the sword of survival. But even
Reason's greatest apologist, Socrates, balanced himself with
equal reverence for mythopoetic knowing. In fact, many
Socratic dialogues point towards the limits of logic and the
essential role of myth. As I sit, a million thoughts cross my
mind, but in keeping with the traditions passed on from

ancient India's great teachers, I attempt to let all of them go, to let them pass like clouds, like water, like time. Needless to say, I often get caught and find myself spinning around one point like a kite trapped by the uppermost twig. But eventually boredom, exhaustion, will-power, or insight—the wind—spins me free and I'm off again.

Sitting gives me a way back to fluctuant, preformed mind, the pregnant atmosphere in which metaphor, intuition, and reason are sparks. Surrounded by a culture of intellectual conquest, I have a preserve of wholeness, a sanctuary in which the wild deer of poetry and song can slip in and out among the trunks of medical cases and conferences. In this sense, sitting is also a nag, tattletale, a wagging finger, reminding me as well as enabling me. I've got to return to the potential, because any one tack is just a shifting situational response to the originless wind.

XII

I sit to anchor my life in certain moods, organize my life around my heart and mind, and to radiate out to others what I find. Though I shake in strong winds, I return to this basic way of living. I can't throw away my boy's ideals and my old man's smile. The easy, soothing comfort and deep relaxation that accompany intense awareness in stillness, peel my life like an onion to deeper layers of truth, which in turn are scoured and soothed until the next layer opens. I sit to discipline my life by what is clear, simple, self-fulfilling, and universal in my heart. There is no end to this job. I have failed to really live many days of my life, but I dive again and again into the plain guidance of self-containment and loving receipt. I sit to find and express simple human love and common decency.

1982

The Therapeutic Action of Vipassana

Vipassana was the meditation practice expounded by the historical Buddha as the direct way to complete liberation from human suffering. Long before the goal is reached, however, the committed ordinary student may gain profound therapeutic benefits from Vipassana. Having practiced this technique religiously for many years, and being a practicing psychiatrist as well, I thought I would describe these therapeutic actions in contemporary psychological language, for the benefit of new and prospective students. All these benefits are potential in the technique; which ones, and how much, accrue to any individual's practice, varies with who one is, where one is coming from, and one's adherence to the technique day after day for a lifetime. I will not attempt to describe the actual practice itself, since that requires the lived experience of a ten-day training course.

I

According to traditional descriptions of the mind as seen through the media of Vipassana, a great part of human mental activity consists of wishes for the future and fears about the future, and desires from the past and fears from the past. The freer the mind is from memories and yearnings, and from desires and hatreds, the more it rests in the present, and the more mental contents come to reflect clear, immediate reality as it is. The technique of meditation allows the controlled release of mental contents, while simultaneously anchoring the student in concrete contemporary reality. This reality-based, equanimous position enables craving and aversion, past and future, to rise to the surface of the mind and to pass away without provoking a reaction. In this way the

mind is deconditioned, and one's life becomes character-
ized by increased awareness, reality-orientation,
non-delusion, self-control, and peace.

Self-Knowledge

This lucid and logical psychology hardly expresses the animated human drama that in fact unfolds whenever anyone
undertakes training in Vipassana. No matter who we are,
our inner lives are less like a box with separate compart-
ments than like a flood-tide on a river. When we sit down to
be still, a seemingly endless stream of memories, wishes,
thoughts, conversations, scenes, desires, dreads, lusts and
emotionally driven pictures of every kind wells up in us,
thousands upon thousands. The clearest, most immediate,
and inescapable effect of meditation is to increase one's self-
knowledge. This may be curious, exciting, and interesting
but it also could be devastating. Taking this into account,
therefore, the technique enables one's vision of one's true
inner life to expand in the structured, protected, controlled,
holding and nurturing environment essential to a safe
launching on high seas.

The qualities of the appropriate environment have been
studied, codified, and transmitted for millennia from teacher
to teacher. Like the map to a traveler, they constitute the
framework of the correctly taught course and facilitate the
qualities of the teacher. A precise adherence to the details
of the technique, and the embracing, generous human love
of the teacher, enable any ordinary person to open the doors
of his or her own heart and mind. Nothing in the human
condition will remain unknown or strange to one who has
sat thus, hour after hour, safely stationed and continuously
aware.

Basic Trust

As a corollary to the expansion of knowledge of one's inner life, then, there is the activation of that basic trust, which
contemporary psychology posits as deriving from the earliest

trust a child extends to the parent who nurtures, warms and feeds it, and which forms the substrate for later intimate human relationships. In the context of Vipassana, this trust operates as the informed adult faith that permits full engagement with the technique without wishful thinking about what magical results it may bring. Such faith must be rooted in thoughtful understanding, reasonable confidence, and the commitment to proceed as directed. Willfulness has to be surrendered, for the platform of knowing is participation.

Integration of the Past

The millions of vignettes, scenes, and anecdotes that flood up from one's personal past, arise to pass away; paradoxically, before they do, one sees who one has been, one knows where one has come from. Even while walking towards the common center, everyone starts from a particular position on the periphery. That position is beyond one's control, because everyone has been conditioned by his past experiences by the thousands, and many of these are not what we would have wished for ourselves. So the present can be grasped, but the past is both elusive yet inescapable. Sitting with it hour after hour necessitates that one come to terms with it. There is no running away, no distraction. Coming to terms with the past, acceptance of what has been, the personal integration of all of oneself without rejection or denial—these are also therapeutic effects of meditation.

Future and Will

Similarly, in spite of any effort to the contrary, the meditator will find himself thinking, preparing, planning and anticipating. Even as this often fanciful activity declines, it enables the meditator to see his real volition emerge. When, as usually happens in life, volition is rapidly followed by action, we find the action more memorable and gripping. Thus retrospectively, we construe life as a series of actions causally linked. We explain ourselves to ourselves based upon what has happened to us and what we did, thus covertly coming to believe ourselves to be dependent products of events, reactors rather than agents.

But the command to ourselves to remain seated, alert, aware, and unmoving, breaks the automaticity of that sequence. The choices and decisions—the motive will in our lives—are pulled out from the shadows to stand on an unobstructed stage. What occurred in fleet milliseconds, to be rapidly followed by loud sequences of actions, now occurs… and that is all. With experience we see how we move, shape, push, and bend with our hearts and minds moment after moment to build the next platform for action. Our future may take us less by surprise, and may ironically require less planning, when we increase our awareness of how our wills mold it. Another therapeutic effect of meditation is to decrease our need to plan, control, and organize the future, because it activates our determination right now to observe, identify, and consciously participate in the thousands of decisions that determine us each day.

Responsibility

Helplessness is one of the most threatening feelings. To be out of control, to be a victim of fate, is universally dreaded. The rites and rituals of organized religion—one of the most widespread phenomena of human culture—are intended to restore a sense of potency, control, and order over events. The wisdom teachings of diverse cultures, on the other hand, eschew reliance on external powers that must be cajoled, coerced, or implored, and teach instead ownership of one's own feelings and actions.

For example, Freud stressed that mental life was not capricious and incomprehensible, but lawful and orderly. Similarly, the Book of Job teaches that apparently arbitrary events can be seen to be caused and meaningful if one maintains the correct attitude; and Jesus' ethics focused on the role of intention and wish in the ultimate destiny of the soul. Existentialism stresses that the individual alone is the maker of his own essence. Viktor Frankl, the existentialist philosopher and psychiatrist, writing from personal experience, claims that even in Auschwitz the individual in essence determined his own fate and had no one else to beseech or blame.

For the meditation student, neither faith nor philosophy, but systematic observation of mind clarifies that every mental event is meaningful, caused, one's own responsibility. Even in fixed conditions, we determine our own attitudes and our responses to those conditions. One mind-moment conditions the next: the more experientially convinced of this we become, the more fully we shoulder responsibility for our own lives. A greater sense of control and responsibility directly follows activation of determination through clarification of will.

Right Concentration and Ethics

But merely "observing the mind" or "watching memories and expectations" is impossible. We cannot simply objectify the very mind that seeks to objectify. There is a technique of meditation that enables us to see the stream of mind-moments rather than be swept along by it. One aspect of the technique is concentration—right concentration. Right concentration is achieved, not by willfully blotting out, repressing, or trampling distraction, but by eliminating distraction's root. So concentration, the treasure of human integrative capacities, which gives coherence and direction to life, cannot be built with a sledgehammer, but requires a feather. When we cease to be distracted in our hearts, so too our minds.

Right concentration depends upon ethical living. Ethics creates inner harmony, the unity of the multiple parts of our being, so that the complexity of a human being attains a point of focus only when the actions of daily life are lined up in the same direction. For right concentration, then, a soft, subtle stimulus is necessary, because the concentration that results from loud demands merely obscures the inner patchwork. Attempting to concentrate upon the difficult-to-concentrate-on produces unavoidable awareness of exactly what is distracting one. So the meditation leads not only to self-awareness, committed participation, integration with and acceptance of one's past, clarity about one's causal role in the future, and a sense of responsibility for one's life, but also to direct experiential knowledge of the basis of ethics. To have peace, we must be at peace.

Distractions from concentration, when neither followed nor suppressed, but seen, are generally desire and fear concerning the past or the future. To concentrate on the subtle, we must dwell in the present and relinquish the multitude of self-enhancing or self-protecting maneuvers that constitute the incessant psychological pressure to fantasy. Then the natural qualities of a mind facing reality become evident.

Self-Control

Concentration—built on harmony, built on ethics, built on an integration with rather than a struggle against reality— occurs not only at the moment-to-moment level but also at the level of life-structure. Order, self-control, and discipline are part of the life of meditation. There is no concentration without them, and they in turn express a focused life. The technique of meditation interlocks with the technique of living; some regulation of sleep, food, sex, and physical motion expresses and enhances awareness and equanimity. But a disciplined life is not a cold or rigid one. As the waves of sentiment wash up on the shore and then—unresponded to—wash away again, we find not flatness of feeling, but depth of emotion, the ocean that underlies the waves.

The frequent misconception that peacefulness is dullness, that detachment is heartlessness, that calm is lethargy, comes from a mind that equates agitation, excitement, and passion with pleasure. But beyond pleasure and displeasure, personal preference, titillation, and taste, are the deep pools of live participation and energy. Rather than static compartmentalization, the disciplines of meditation allow full emotional access, spontaneous and generous flows of compassionate, empathetic feeling.

Conflict Resolution

From the ancient religious masters like the Buddha, Jesus, St. Paul, Krishna, and Rumi to modern theologians like Tillich, Buber, and Eliade, human wholeness has been considered the goal and meaning of religion. Freud claimed that conflict or disunity was the cause of neurosis, and post-Freudian psychology has intensely studied integrative aspects of the personality, such as identity. Meditation is a direct method of decreasing psychological conflict through its prescriptive ethical codes, its integration of past and future, its elucidation of self-responsibility, concentration, and will. Conflict resolution could be said to be the main thrust of the practice.

Yet life is dynamic. There is no final static formula that can encase the fluid ocean of reality that we experience as commitments, goals, meanings, and concerns. So meditation often heightens awareness of existential conflicts as it decreases the level of division, fragmentation, or disunity. There is no automatic drive pedal in Vipassana, no end to renewed right effort and real challenge.

History and Community

Vipassana meditation comes from people of the past, and is part of contemporary lives. It passes from person to person—not from books or lectures or mass media. The depth of feeling created by the practice is not an abstraction, a religious ideal. Friendship, companionship, actual human warmth are part of the technique. This is not chattering sociability, but the mutual respect and support of those who see the predawn stars side-by-side.

Just as the practice is shared now, it has been shared across time. A sense of heritage, lineage, history is an inevitable experience of the Vipassana student. Awareness of one's personal history increases one's sense of personal

integrity, and experience of the meaning of human history
is a critical element of all deep psychological healing. Like
our language, our meditation places us in a trans-temporal
human community. Membership in generative continuity is
a sweet antidote to self-aggrandizement. The finest plant
has to be modest in the presence of the soil. Philosophical
meaning is an idle abstraction to those whose hands actually reach across generations.

Time and Change

Location within the transmission of generations is only one
way that Vipassana opens the student's eyes to the reality of
time and change. Improving the student's capacity to look
directly at the reality of impermanence, flux, emptiness, and
death is at the core of the practice. The technique involves
seeing reality fully, but only after appropriate preparation.
Confrontation with pain and dissolution, however, is a universal human experience; Vipassana enables that meeting to
occur with equanimity. So the technique contains an irony:
the starker our confrontation with reality, the deeper our
equanimity; the deeper our equanimity, the more superficial desires and fears peel off like onion skins and the closer
we come to the core anxieties of human existence.

Physical immobility is core human fear (everyone has
had the dream of paralysis, being unable to run, unable to
speak); Vipassana prepares us to face it. Physical pain is a
core human fear (some psychiatrists consider it the bedrock of all fear); Vipassana leads us into it, and out of it.
Loneliness is a core human fear; Vipassana leads us to trust,
community, faith, but also to profound solitude in silence,
and we can learn to turn that ice into a cool drink for a hot
mind. Ancient and modern theories of the human heart frequently point to death as the node, the point where character
forms, where knowledge is tested, and where the deepest
anxieties take their root. Socrates, of course, considered
philosophy the art of dying; a large body of contemporary

psychiatric theory echoes that, as does the technique of Vipassana meditation.

One reason the mind is always in flight, daydreaming, thinking, planning, remembering, is that concentration on immediate physical reality will inevitably clarify the feared truth: the body is decaying right now, every moment, irreversibly. One of the paradoxes of the Vipassana technique is that the deep physical concentration and relaxation, the exquisite luminescent peace, will lead to the core of dread... which in turn can be experienced as a simple sweet truth like night followed by dawn, hunger followed by food, tiredness followed by sleep, rest followed by morning stars. A mind that returns to the body knows both the limitations of that body, and the vibrating universal energy flowing from form to form.

Bodily Integration

Vipassana is not merely a mental activity. It happens in a body, and is more analogous to learning to ride a bicycle than to learning to read. Awareness of all of our body all of the time is one of the keys to the practice. Thoughts and emotions inevitably have counterparts in bodily events. So systematic awareness of ourselves requires awareness of how we sit, eat, sleep, think, and feel directly through the body itself. Emotions that were formerly placeless ghosts in the halls of ourselves can be experienced as producing specifically located sensations in the skin, heart, eyes, scalp. Desires and fears that drove us half-consciously to a ceaseless flurry of comfort-seeking can be found to affect the bodily process at deep and subtle levels. Even the past and future, to which we previously did obeisance as awesome external powers, will be found in us, in our vibrating physical selves, as excitation, hunger, and lethargy.

Since all bodies decay, dissolve, and pass away, physical pain and illness are inevitable universal human experiences; and Vipassana can quickly disperse a student's covert belief in his own invulnerability. But another fraction of suffering stems from ignorance: reactions blindly stored in muscle spasms, engorged overconsumptions, chronic constrictions of self-chastisement, recoiling and clamping down, in blood vessels or intestines. Deepened bodily awareness is the best method of observing the living organic root of thought and emotion, and may also reorder bodily habits, occasionally effecting cures of psychosomatic headaches, gastro-intestinal spasms, and the like.

Relationship

The experience of ceaseless, continuous change in every molecule of the body in every moment casts life in a different perspective. Meanings and purposes organized around oneself alone are clearly pointless. In every millisecond life rises out of the whole and returns to it again, rearising fresh, new, different. We exist in the whole, like flecks of spray thrown up momentarily out of the ocean. What is the point of those self-aggrandizing efforts we were so recently, so strenuously pursuing?

Contemporary psychiatry has expressed a renewed interest in the way a person organizes a sense of self in relation to other selves; in Vipassana we experience directly the arsenal of attitudes, postures, lectures, and reactions we all elaborate to create and sustain the image of our own impregnable, eternal, inviolate existence—and how doomed a defense that is. The psychology of the self is a study of building castles of granite on quicksand. That static self that we yearn for, demand, and forever insist upon is a plastic sticker pasted over flow, process, interaction, relation. Without preaching or ideation, the direct experience available through meditation washes away our entitlement, grandiosity, self-preoccupation, and incorporative greed. This cleansing is particularly refreshing to people from modern Western cultures, which have been called cultures of self-absorption.

Truth

Truth is not content, but a process. It means an attitude of expectation and freshness, a willingness to mentally restructure again and again. Vipassana meditation could be described as the technique of living by the truth. The truth in this sense is not a school, and idea, a doctrine. It doesn't imply an "us" and a "them." It doesn't mean that people living in other ways don't have the truth. The practice simply points to one technique whereby a person's life can stake itself out to the process of exploration every day, day after day, up to death itself, which hopefully can be greeted with the same query: objectively, what is the nature of the reality of my mind and body at this moment? Science, philosophy, or any open-minded living share in this truth. Vipassana is one well-tried and proven technique, and it contains the paradox of an objective approach to the subjective, and inquiry into the nature of ourselves. Truth is not just the "high-falutin'," and the living attempt to express oneself truthfully in fleeting conventional moments is one of the finest tools to pry loose the door of the over-defended self.

Human Love

What does the experience of meditation reveal in the human heart? Underneath the self-protective shields of anger, aggression, possession, and control lies the well of clear, simple, loving, energetic, vital life. Generosity, compassion, and human love are not virtues, but attributes. Everybody yearns to feel love, engagement, and the light of truth. But fear and caution encourage us to continually take detours. We imagine that one more wall, one more lock will keep us safe. Practicing Vipassana means practicing the direct action of human love. It crystallizes the yearning in us, the call, so that we feel ourselves in possession of the jewel for which we had been searching.

II

There are a few questions I am frequently asked when people find out that a psychiatrist has chosen to root his life in meditation.

Do I teach patients to mediate? Definitely not. As a secular professional, I don't impose practices or world-views (beyond the broadly sanctioned general ethics of the dominant culture) on patients who come to me. No one is value-free, but a psychiatrist must be ready to listen to and nurture many ways of being a human being. Central to the profession is the capacity to follow another person's need and lead. People who are called to the practice of meditation will come to it, so I neither hide it nor flaunt it. A number of patients who have seen me have come to know about my way of life; most haven't, knowing that as a professional I offer not a person to emulate or admire, but a treatment that enables them to be more fully and deeply themselves.

In my own mind I imagine that the truth has many facets but one essence. I respect the facets. In any case, a psychiatrist frequently is the interface for the exercise of a bitter cynicism, not to mention the panorama of perversions, rages, paralyzing confusions, and so many other phenomena of hurt lives. People start in different places and require various modes of help—in this light psychiatry, too, is also very limited.

Then do I use meditation at all in my work? Yes—it *is* my work, heart and core. For in all those variations of human pain, I see myself as I have seen myself as I sit. There is little in the phenomenology of my patients' lives that is not in mine also. Meditation has greatly enriched my empathy, and my vision of what it is to be a human being: the fear and anxiety and dependency and exhaustion; the desperation and defeat and revival and acceptance; the vision and work and delight and struggle; the doggedness and creativity and appreciation and gratitude. By having experienced my own deeper, truer nature I know more; by experiencing those vibrations in every hour of my daily work with people, I have been able to open more fully, to receive and hold, to drop defenses of my own, to really listen, to really understand.

Interestingly, Freud described a similar process; he said that the psychoanalyst has not only to turn off his conscious thinking, but to open his own being like a receiver to the transmitting antennae of the patient. I can hold more, and it is clear to me that I've been given more to hold. But practicing psychiatry is more than being nice, and I've also learned from meditation how long, difficult, demanding, and very painful it is to face reality, to break old molds.

Is meditation really effective? I think so—but only with devoted practice. While I have seen many lives, my own included, send down taproots into the simple, common, human decency that transcends theology, philosophy, and psychology, I have also known many people who have meditated for periods of time and then just tumbled on. Meditation cannot be practiced casually alone in the bedroom; there must be real training. But there is also an essential requirement for disciplined regularity in daily life. According to the Buddha, the ultimate source of human suffering is ignorance, which includes within itself a resistance to knowing the truth that can set us free. The moment we turn away is when the bird glides into its nest. When we skip, miss, forget, can't make it—that's when the unconscious controls us. Systematic choiceless routine is essential for opening the mind to observation, for in one small lapse the large source of that lapse is obscured. If you draw a water bucket steadily up from a well for five minutes, and then let go for one split second... the result is clear.

Although the practice of Vipassana is not a religion in the sense of buying into or swallowing dogma, ritual, or blind faith, I think it is critical to practice "religiously": that is, with devoted centrality of commitment. Meditation as a desultory practice, an amusement, an occasional hobby in a cluttered life, has little effect, and may stir up more confusion than it relieves. Unfortunately I have seen intermittent, self-directed meditation used to hide from reality, to devalue painful dilemmas, and in one instance, to aggrandize the self to the point of madness and suicide.

Vipassana references itself to universal human wisdom rather than to particular cultural forms. It is nonsectarian in thought. Its framework is mirrored whenever people ponder the art of living. For example, Thoreau wrote, in Massachusetts, in the nineteenth century: "Renew thyself completely each day; do it again, and again, forever again.... To affect the quality of the day, that is the highest art... no method or discipline can supersede the necessity of being forever on the alert...."

The potential therapeutic actions of Vipassana include increased self-knowledge, deepened human trust and participation, integration with and acceptance of one's past, deepened activation of one's will, an increased sense of responsibility for one's own fate; greater concentration, deepened ethical commitments, firm yet flexible life structures and disciplines, fluid access to deeper streams of feeling and imagery, expanded historical and contemporary community; prepared confrontation with core realities such as time, change, death, loss, pain leading to an eventual diminution of dread, anxiety, and delusion; fuller body-mind integration, decreased narcissism, and a fuller panorama of character strengths such as generosity, compassion, and human love. Each student starts at a different place, and progresses individually; there is no magic and no guarantee.

III

To consider meditation from the standpoint of its therapeutic actions is only one way of describing this technique of living. Seen from another direction, meditation transcends the merely therapeutic, the way that the water of the planet exceeds its mere thirst-quenching property, the way the sun exceeds its life and warmth-giving qualities, the way a timeless poem exceeds the personal pleasure that we may individually extract from it. We are part of a reality that is more than a cure for our personalities. The point is not towards ourselves, but towards everything else.

The entire description of Vipassana meditation via its therapeutic actions clarifies some points, but obscures a very central one. While meditation is therapeutic—enhancing many other human qualities—it has intrinsic value as an activity in itself. Art may help us to appreciate life; it also expresses human nature's artful heart, eye, and hand. Meditation is most therapeutic when it is not looked upon for therapeutic effect, but is put into practice as an end in itself, and expression of an aspect of human nature. That aspect is not a single attribute, like one slice of a pie, but a sustaining, synthesizing, creative force in all other aspects, like the heat that baked the pie. It is more like the bony skeleton than like one limb. So meditation expresses something about the integrated process of a person, rather than being merely a means to ends in other spheres of life.

Meditation expresses that aspect of us which can receive: the nonselective embracing receptor. We can know ourselves as member cells of an integrated whole. Occasionally a person will feel this way during special hours of special days: watching a sunset from the rimrocks of a sandstone canyon in a wilderness of pinyon pine and ancient ruins. These moments are inspirational, serendipitous interludes. Meditation entails the systematic cultivation of this formative human potential as a lifelong centering enterprise. While some activation of this receptive, interpenetrative, non-judgmental mode is the foundation of any art or science, any significant engagement of the world, it has been most exquisitely expressed by certain writers, like Tagore, Whitman, Thoreau, the Socratic dialogues, Chinese and Japanese Zen poets, and the nameless authors of many classical Pāli and Sanskrit texts from ancient India.

This equanimous, aware, unfiltered, receptivity is the *sine qua non* of religious experience (as opposed to mere religious membership or affiliation). Opening it up makes us feel whole and alive just as eating does. There is no need to rationalize supper as being therapeutic; it is an essential expression of life itself. Similarly, to open up and know with our being is not health-giving, but life-giving. I have come to believe that meditation activates the process underlying all religious life when looked at for what lies inside the specific cultural or religious formulas, that it contains the essential ingredient of all the pleomorphic panoply of religion—based on studying the great students of the psychology of religion: William James, Carl Jung, Paul Tillich, Erik Erikson, Jerome Frank, Mircea Eliade, et al.

But when we open to receive the whole, a great darkness floods in too. Our previously selective, circumscribed flashlight cannot illumine it alone. We can no longer exclude the devouring mouths of time, the Hitlerian epochs cauterizing living limbs of whole centuries, civilizations, peoples; our fears for ourselves and all we love seem like ephemeral flecks of spray foaming up and vanishing endlessly on a boundless ocean. Human culture itself, with its religious and artistic and scientific geniuses, has provided candles, torches, even suns for us, that reveal miraculously the dry land between the seas. Vipassana is one of these. It is a technique that enables us to hear the wisdom of life itself, contained in our organism just like the wisdom of hunger, revealing the deepening shaft of vision, determination, more indomitable skill and gentleness in service of the life in which we live. Inside us and around us is the maker for whom we care. Vipassana meditation is one way to activate an enduring, sustaining love in the web of all contacts.

Students who undertake training in this discipline will find themselves walking into a large, dark hall at 4:00 a.m. Around them will be many silent, seated, erect friends along the way, men and women, professors and unemployed travelers, lawyers and mothers, who have been there, morning after morning, day after day, for ten days. Darkness will fade, there will be fewer stars, the crescent moon will glow alone, birds will unroll a curtain of life before the new day, and then depart. The hall will be light, yet still, motionless, silent;

a chant will begin, whose twenty-five-hundred-year-old words simply point us towards the best in us; and even slightly bleary and dry, the students may motionlessly reach up and pluck an invisible jewel of immeasurable worth.

1986

Vipassana Meditation: Healing the Healer

Vipassana is an ancient meditation technique that is still practiced today, and that can help healing professionals themselves. As a practicing and teaching psychiatrist, I have been aided, through my practice of Vipassana, to deepen my autonomy and self knowledge at the same time that I have augmented my ability to be a professional anchor to others in the tumult of their lives. I have written about my experience and understanding of meditation in earlier chapters. Here I want to focus on the healers' healing: why nutritionists, chiropractors, yoga teachers, family practitioner-physicians, psychologists and psychiatrists of my acquaintance have all been able to grow in their personal and professional lives while practicing Vipassana.

Vipassana touches the common ground of healing. It is acceptable and relevant to healers of diverse disciplines because it is free of dogma, experientially based, and focused on human suffering and relief. It contains the healing element from which the various molecules of our helping professions are built.

What, after all, must we do and be to heal ourselves, and to have energy to heal others? I believe the answer to this question is both obvious and universally acknowledged among healers of differing theoretical orientations.

We must see deeply into ourselves, our personal fears and prejudices and conventions and opinions, so that we may stand thoughtfully, clear-sightedly on reality. We must be able to differentiate the accidents of our birth, culture, and particular conditionings from the universal and the timeless truths.

We must live balanced, full lives, that sweep up the breadth and depth of what is potential in us as human beings; yet at the same time we must focus with discipline, determination, endurance, and continuity on what is central, essential, critical.

We must love, not just those who by accident or choice abut upon our lives, but love the potential for awakening that stirs within every life form, so that we can glimpse in the turmoil around us the possibility of an upward-reaching nature. We must accept, bow, acknowledge that death will lead each of us, each of our patients away, but we must spark faith, hope for this next moment's luminosity in those who are pained, defeated, cynical, withered.

We must restrain our own lusts, impulses, needs, yet we must nourish ourselves so that self-containment does not culminate in dryness, but enables the fullness of the fountain of inner life.

We must walk the path from ignorance to knowledge, from doubt to clarity, from conviction to discovery. We must start anew every day, without accretions of doctrines and conclusions, like fledglings in the springtime of knowledge.

Vipassana is a way that a healer can ascend while carrying the burdens and demands of professional life.

Vipassana meditation was discovered twenty-five centuries ago by Gotama, the Buddha. In the language that he spoke, the meaning of the word Vipassana is insight, to see things as they really are. Although Vipassana contains the core of what later has been called Buddhism, it is not an organized religion, requires no conversion, and is open to students of any faith, nationality, color, or background. In its pure form, which can still be found and followed today, it is a non-sectarian art of living in harmony with the laws of nature. It is the ethical and social path that derives from an exploration of nature within the framework of one's own mind and body. Vipassana's goals are liberation from suffering, and spiritual transcendence. It leads to inner peace, which those who practice it learn to share with others. Heal-ing—not disease cure, but the essential healing of human suffering—is the purpose of Vipassana.

The passage of centuries obscured Vipassana in most of the countries to which it had originally spread, but in some lands it was preserved. In a few places the original practice of the Buddha in its hard simplicity was handed down in pure form from teacher to teacher across thousands of years. For centuries it remained unknown and unavailable to the West because of language and cultural barriers. Only recently, as Eastern Vipassana teachers themselves learned Western languages and ways, has the practice begun to spread around the world.

Credit for this is due to a Burmese layman, the late Saya-gyi U Ba Khin, who was a master Vipassana teacher, and who also progressed in worldly affairs until he became Accountant General of newly independent Burma in 1947. U Ba Khin was familiar with British culture and language, and was free of ethnocentricity. He accepted as his disciple a Burmese-born Indian, S.N. Goenka, who has followed his teacher's tradition, and Buddha's tradition, of transcending the barriers of localized custom, sectarian religion, ethnic chauvinism, or other parochial affiliations. Through the work of Mr. Goenka and his assistant teachers in the past decade, Vipassana has spread worldwide.

Vipassana is taught in ten-day courses that require students to live in silence and full-time meditation. Each course is taught in an ambiance that duplicates and facilitates the goals of the practice. No conversation, reading, writing, radios, telephone calls, or other distractions are permitted. Students begin their course with vows to adhere to high moral values for the ten days: specifically to refrain from taking any life, to refrain from any intoxicants or sexual activity, to avoid lying or stealing. The students then progress for three and a half days through a preliminary, concentrative meditation which focuses on breath. From that they proceed to Vipassana proper: insight into the nature of the entire mind and body phenomenon. The ethical, restrained atmosphere and the concentrative background make six and a half days of silent practice of Vipassana in noble silence an intense, profound, often life-transforming experience.

Vipassana, as handed down from the Buddha through the chain of teachers to U Ba Khin and Mr. Goenka, has a unique feature among meditation practices, one that makes it particularly relevant to either somatically or psychologically oriented healers. It focuses on the absolute interconnection between mind and body. Through disciplined attention, students learn to observe directly within themselves that their bodies are constantly filled with myriad shifting sensations. These sensations in turn condition the mind. In fact, most mental life is a product of bodily life. If this last sentence sounds overstated, and you feel you are really your "mind" or "soul", try an experiment: chop off your head. Or, if that sounds extreme, instead try a Vipassana meditation course; it will take you on an observation-based, self-exploratory journey, to the common root of mind and body. A ten-day Vipassana experience will shatter your dualism, and replace it with a revolutionary vision of the unity of mind-body and its role in the unconscious origins of a sense of self.

During a ten-day meditation course, the unbroken atmosphere of hard work coupled to a supportive ambience enables a flood of personal memories, hopes, and reveries to enter the student's consciousness for the first time. Along with awareness of this liberated flood of mental life, Vipassana also raises into consciousness awareness of an equally compelling stream of bodily sensations that constitute the physical level of life. The interconnection of these twin streams of becoming, mental and physical, lies at the root of our experience of ourselves. Every thought has a specific sensation connected to it. Every bodily sensation is connected to a thought. Usually, these two streams of life seem disconnected, autonomous, even at odds, because we haven't

observed them systematically and carefully enough. Awareness of the psycho-somatic junction depends upon
unbroken, introverted concentration. Once we have established meditative mindfulness, we can observe directly the
manner in which our thoughts become embodied.

Suffering springs from ignorance of our true nature.
Insight, truth—experiential truth—frees us. The right path
of life—not simply the path of one particular form of spiri-
tuality, but the path of all healing, including self-healing and
other-healing, the path that points to the origin and elimination of suffering—becomes as clear as observations from
a mountaintop.

Through Vipassana, we can see that we ourselves create
the reality in which we live. Therefore within ourselves is
the way, and the only way, out of suffering. What a person
calls "self" is a mental-physical structure, an impersonal
stream of transitory events, each one caused by the one before. Like any other natural phenomenon, we consist of a
cloud of particles, a bundle of energy, responding to the scientific laws that run the universe. These scientific laws
operate not only upon electrons, protons, and neutrons, but
also upon our thoughts, feelings, judgements and sensations.
At the subtlest level, our minds and bodies interconnect at
the juncture where the physical arising and vanishing of the
matter in our bodies is in contact with our minds. Events
and thoughts that impinge upon our senses create changes
in our somatic sensations. Our judgement of and reaction
to this somatic sensory substrate form the mental-physical
complexes we come to identify as ourselves. The constant
mental reaction to somatic pain and pleasure conditions our
unconscious definition of who and what we are.

The depth and power of our identification with the sensations of our bodies cannot be overestimated. I remember
listening to a group of psychoanalysts discussing the Arab
oil embargo in the early 1970s. At that time, long gas lines
were forming, cars could hardly be used on weekends, and

the availability of winter fuel oil was uncertain. The American way of life wasn't threatened—surely there was no danger to balanced judicial opinion, legislative government, freedom of thought, assembly, or press. Yet in the reaction of Americans, a terror and rage was provoked. The psychoanalysts standing in the medical school reception room schemed out loud how to augment their own ration of auto fuel, how to insure no disruption of their warmth and convenience. The note beneath their cocky self-assertion was—it seemed to me—terror. I thought to myself that these elder American healers may have been freed of oedipal problems by their psychoanalytic insight, but they remained prey to panicky dependence upon the somatic opulence of American society. Shortly after, the American president declared the Persian Gulf doctrine, which implied that America would risk nuclear holocaust of the earth if its oil supply were threatened. Consumptive fury-to-death underlies the behavior of leading healers and leading statesmen. The core of this fury is aversion to somatic sensations like cold, or the irritation of delay. Rather than feel them, we would risk toppling the whole tower of blocks. Each one of us who is honest will find a bit of this violently reactive petulance in him or herself.

Still, this represents only the macro-behavior associated with gross sensations like cold or hunger. What Vipassana reveals is an increasingly subtle level, where thousands of sensations are signaling throughout our bodies continuously. At the level of covert, unconscious thought-behavior, we are continuously impelled to respond as if these biochemical clouds of molecular events in our bodies were ourselves. Vipassana meditation enables us to experience the deep vibratory substrate of unconscious mental clinging or aversion to physical events in the body, and to elevate these reactions into consciousness. Through this process, the meditator can transform primitive somatic self-identifications that might have led to suffering, into awareness and free choice.

Vipassana opens our two eyes: the eye of awareness of the root of our sense of self in bodily sensations, and the eye of equanimity; the capacity to observe a myriad of subtle sensations, and their mental counterparts, without judgment or reaction, based on the realization that they are all ephemeral, transitory, not "self". The new vision produced by the practice of awareness and equanimity results in graduation from the previously unconscious, gripping identification with somatic pleasure and pain. Vipassana is the path of transcendence of the pleasure principle.

A ten-day intensive Vipassana course is only the start of a long journey. Each person consists of an aggregation of countless thousands of conditioned emotional and behavioral reactions. Some are incidental, trivial. Some form significant complexes: rigid, stereotyped attitudes, beliefs, and behaviors, conditioned by events and reactions in the past, that fire repetitively in fixed, historically conditioned patterns, in spite of the fact that life calls for thoughtful, specific, flexible responses. Modern western psychotherapies are built upon the delineation, analysis, and elimination of these complexes. The psychotherapies are very similar to Vipassana in some of their methods and goals. Both enable healing through systematic self-awareness, self-knowledge, and freedom from past conditioning. Meditation and psychotherapy to some extent represent the convergence that is found throughout organic evolution: common problems which impel common solutions. Vipassana meditation differs from the psychotherapies, in its basis of specific ethical values, its particular cultivation of mindfulness of sensations, and its specification of a lifelong path evolving the transcendent. Healing is only one aspect of Vipassana, which is a broader approach to life itself.

Vipassana is not merely an exercise to be performed in the special environment of a meditation retreat. When a ten-day course is over, meditators take the tool home with them. The path of Vipassana is a continuous, disciplined pursuit of this experiential gnosis throughout life.

Although we imagine we are responding to people and events, we are actually responding to the covert fluxes of bio-physical transformations triggered in us by those externals. Vipassana heals through ethical dedication, lifelong introspective discipline, self-knowledge and self-responsibility. Events are at best only partly under my control. My reactions, however, occur within the field of my physical life and self-identification, and ultimately are under my own control. I suffer not because of what has happened to me, but because I was unable to detach myself from the reactions to those events within my mind-body. Objectivity is freedom from suffering. Detachment from internal reactivity releases energy for giving. External fate may be imposed upon each of us, but psychological fate is a matter of consciousness and decision.

The path of Vipassana is a human capacity and a personal choice. It points towards a tranquil wisdom that transcends the automaticity of animal existence. Rather than reducing human life to a psycho-physical machine, this meditation exposes the ignorance of unconscious reactivity and releases the spirit of wisdom, virtue and illumination. The meditator becomes free to live for higher values, richer goals: loving kindness, sympathetic joy, compassion and peacefulness. Fear and yearning give way to choice, ardor, and faith in the human potential.

In this meditation practice, there is an embrace of whole life. No area is too trivial to explore. There is no blind faith, no divine intervention, no passive dependent pleading that will elevate us. Meditation practice is the vigorous and detailed pursuit of one's own wisdom. Vipassana makes us self-responsible, because it reveals, through self-observation, how we become our reactions and values. The path consists of making every thought in every moment a seed of equanimity that will bear the fruit of love and peace.

Healers will recognize in this aspect of the practice the basis for self-responsibility in symptom formation and symptom reversal. They will engage a world view that is natural and scientific, free of dogmas or authoritarianism. They can enter a way that is the authentic transmission of the ancient East, time-tested, genuine, validated across the centuries by the actual practice and experience of millions of lives. Yet at the same time Vipassana is free of gurus, exotic costumes, or ethnocentric rituals. Instead of blind dependence on the teacher, Vipassana encourages respect and gratitude for the technique itself. Incidentally, there is no fee for the teaching; the ring of authenticity is confirmed as the students realize that U Ba Khin, S.N. Goenka, and all his assistants receive no payment for the teaching, which is handed on, person to person, on a charitable, spiritual basis. The teachers all earn their living elsewhere. The courses and centers where Vipassana is taught run on voluntary donations only.

The long silent hours of a Vipassana meditation course bring to the surface of the mind its previously repressed and hidden contents. The result is a deep exposure of one's personal history, one's inner life. The healer will find deepened self-knowledge as a result, and deeper empathy with the suffering of others. I know of no greater humanizer than exposure to our own life story in the unexpurgated edition. Another benefit for healers is greater respect for the multiplicity of healing modalities. Instead of needing to defend one's own discipline against others—psychiatry is right, acupuncture is wrong; chiropractic is right, yoga is wrong— one can appreciate how thought, feeling, judgment, choice and action are the common cause of suffering and the common way out. The walls of our own world are built by how we think, how we act, how we give. The healing modalities differ in where they intervene. They are efficacious to the extent that they operate on these core, universal variables. They are deceptive to the extent that they obscure one or more of these variables.

Thus nutrition that leads to social energy can be clearly differentiated from gluttony and epicureanism. Exercise that produces awareness and vitality can be clearly differentiated from body-building vanity or blind competitive aggression. Treatments that augment self-responsibility can be differentiated from those that foster dependency. Through Vipassana, we can transcend body-mind, or even East-West, dualism, and shake hands with ethical rootedness, cultivated mindfulness, and wisdom in all its enduring forms. Empathy, firmness, example, endurance, open mindedness, and a gateway to higher values are found in every worthwhile black bag.

II

In my professional work as a supervisor of psychiatrists-in-training and as a psychiatrist to other psychiatrists, psychologists, social workers, physicians and health professionals, I have become acquainted with a syndrome that could be called "the wounded healer." The wounded healer functions as a high-quality professional. He or she is typically well-trained, diligent, self-educating, and reliably kind and knowledgeable in dealing with patients. But, inside, known only to themselves, and carefully concealed from others, the wounded healer feels alone, frightened, anxious, depressed. His or her professional attainments are genuine, and form excellent compensations for experiences of deprivation earlier in life. The wounded healer is typically an avoidant, proper, lonely person, who gives generously professionally in order to get the human contact of which he or she feels otherwise deprived. He or she is apt to hide deep feelings of hurt even from his or her spouse. The wounded healer permits him- or herself to become a patient only cautiously, sometimes waiting decades for the right healer to come along. As professionals themselves, they judge carefully. Their progress in psychotherapy is slow, because rather than having a single issue or focus, what they seek is the nurturing and sustained attention of therapy itself. They want cure less than they want participation, membership, an adoptive parent to heal and hold them as their original parents, for any one of various reasons, could not.

Originally, when I was first sought out by one or two established psychiatrists to be their psychiatrist, I was flattered by their estimation of me and I considered their problems in a purely individual light. Over the years, as the treatment of the wounded professional has become my major activity, I have come to understand that the problem is not only individual. The wounded healer, I now believe, represents something essential at the core of healing. Freud and Jung insisted that analysts be analyzed. All people need healing, most particularly healers. The wounded healer will have his or her own unique constellation of individual and personal problems, but he or she also experiences the pain of pain. The very vulnerability and compassion that sets the healer on that lifelong journey, coupled to the constant exposure to human suffering, requires a treatment of its own. I have come to understand that the wounded healer is so cautious, circumspect and careful in selecting his or her own healer not merely out of pride, shame, professional scruples or trained judgment but also because he or she seeks personal healing that respects the previous truth of his or her own suffering. In the words of the Argentine potter and poet Antonio Porchia: "He who has seen everything empty itself is close to knowing what everything is filled with." A wounded healer's pain is not only a problem, but a valuable source of empathy and insights. It is the magnet that draws healers towards the fate of healing. The wounded healer brings to his or her healer not merely blind pain, but the kernel of noble suffering.

Noble suffering is human misery that drives towards insight, determination, release. It is the knowledge that suffering is existential. The deep note of noble suffering is what differentiates true healing from superficial patch-ups and fraudulent elixirs. The wounded healer is a person suffering from a deep, human, personal pain, who is able to perceive in his or her own plight the kernels of the universal truth about all pain and all plights, and who is accordingly sensitized to, and activated by, a lifelong calling to heal.

Noble suffering is the pathology beneath existential dismay which meditation dissects clearly into sight. It is the recognition that life is a gift, and pain.

Born with neurons, we will feel pain. Born with hearts, we will cry. The gift of life is conditional: only if we use it can we have it, and to use it means to realize that the pains and sorrows of existence are not merely circumstantial, but are intrinsic to tissue and to mind. Noble suffering is distress that serves as provocation to relinquish ourselves. Soon the trees, birds, school children and grandparents will be felt as crying out for your healing emanations that convey: "this hurting and inconstant self is not really you."

When I came to understand myself as a variant of the wounded healer, I appreciated Vipassana more deeply. Its age-old tradition of friendship and comradeship with all living things—squirrels, lakes, atmospheric presences, high school teachers and writers—helped me feel surrounded by infinities of helpers for my own consternation, and recipients of my skills and affections. Oceans of beings swim with me, reach out to me, count on me to whisper inspiring exhortations in their ears.

Many contemporary psychotherapies and healings seem to me to be blindly organized around success, happiness, bourgeois attainment: two cars, two children, two houses, two wives, as if the whole world were invented in New Jersey and limited to the next twenty years. In Vipassana I had located a healing where my life wasn't organized around the opulence of my vacations or the applause and kudos I received. The path begins with the attitude that suffering can have a noble, enlightening function, and expands to incorporate new perspectives on time, space, our kinships beyond tactile immediacies.

In Vipassana, my birth and death on the shore of the mysterious ocean of the universe is a common bond to all beings. Vipassana is an ideal healing for healers, I believe, because it validates and affirms the direction given to life by conscious confrontation with the dismay that accompanies birth and death. Vipassana does not aim to palliate pain with comfort. Its goal is not health. Every person becomes sick and dies. The goal of Vipassana is the realization that the self is an illusory prison which leads to birth, death, suffering. The sense of a self is an illusion based upon the conditioning exerted by somatic sensations upon the mind. Vipassana meditation brings into the open the existential link between sensations, self-concepts, and suffering, and permits a reawakening to the world beyond one's self. It operates at the common root where individual, isolated anguish opens out into the stream of undivided, selfless love. It heals by activating virtues that transcend self-success, self-pleasure, self-life. The meditator steps out into that which exists beyond the transient boundaries of body and mind.

Do I refer all my patients to Vipassana then? How—why—can I value and practice psychiatry? Vipassana meditation courses are not of interest to everyone. Some people may be too agitated or preoccupied to benefit—many kinds of help exist for many reasons. Some individuals may have preconceptions and prejudices that would keep them from meditating; others may have addictions or anxieties that would preclude their facing the removal from familiar environments that meditation courses require. Some simply rotate through hemispheres of different affinities. There can be no conversion, exhortation, arm-twisting or imposition on this respectful and non-harmful path. The ten-day course is hard work. A lifetime on the path is rarer, harder work. It requires no exceptional intelligence, no athletic skill, no particular cultural background, but it does require character strength and a call.

Vipassana meditators who continue to walk the path for their lifetime come from all walks of life; of course, the vast majority are not themselves healers. Some are illiterate, some poor, some old, some crippled, some physically ill. Indian peasant farmers, German sociologists, Australian carpenters and French psychotherapists practice this way of life. Like the image of Noah's ark, every kind is represented. But there are some requirements, though they tend to be intangible.

Meditators must "have the seed". Like the life of any seed, the seed of meditation eludes the microscope of words: is it basic good faith; or a sense of determination; or enough miseries and losses to have to keep going; or an unfathomable curiosity about their own true nature; or an intuition of values that transcend immediate life; or a yearning for peace; or a recognition of the limitations of mundane routines? It was said by the Buddha that at the heart of the path lies *ahimsa*, non-harmfulness. Is it an inkling of the infinite curative value that this most treasured and elusive cumulative virtue provides, that constitutes the seed? In any case, a life of meditation is a path for those who hear the call, seek it out, and sit down to observe. Some may not seek it, some may not value it, some may not tolerate it, some may have other valuable paths to take.

The French psychoanalyst, Jacques Lacan, wrote, "Psychoanalysis may accompany the patient to the ecstatic limit of the 'thou art that,' in which is revealed to him the cipher of his mortal destiny, but it is not in our mere power as practitioners to bring him to that point where the real journey begins." Vipassana meditation is based on one thing: "This is suffering; this is the way out of suffering." It is the path where the real journey begins. It is a healing by observation of and participation in the laws of nature. Even the stars are born and die, but beyond the transiency of the world there is an eternal that each of us can travel towards. Vipassana heals by focusing onto particular pain the invisible spectrum of the universal.

1990

Vipassana Meditation:
A Unique Contribution to Mental Health

Can everyone benefit from a ten-day Vipassana course? Are there people who should avoid these courses, temporarily or permanently? Can some types of problems, that are understood in the West as psychiatric disorders, be cured by Vipassana meditation? Would Vipassana help someone more than psychotherapy would?

I am asked these questions recurrently, but have found myself unable to answer them adequately in the moment that they are posed, because the questions are too general to be accurately applied to particular people in the context of their specific life circumstances. To accurately answer these questions, it is necessary to have a proper understanding of Vipassana's unique contribution to mental health. Then each person's circumstance can be reflected upon in the light of right understanding. In this article, instead of glib generalizations, I would like to describe in some detail what Vipassana can and cannot contribute to mental health.

1) Vipassana is Unique

Vipassana meditation is unique in many ways. As the meditation that was practiced by the Buddha and that led to his liberation, it is the cause underlying his subsequent historical role—it is the second womb through which he was reborn enlightened. No other person, or system of self-development, has influenced so many hundreds of millions of people, across so many historical eras, among so many nations and cultures, in such an unambiguous manifestation of compassion, harmony and peace.

Historically, before the Buddha, all religions were a mixture of moral injunction, propitiation of gods, magic, superstition, and ethnocentrism. The Buddha brought forth the idea of a limitless community, not based on language, ethnicity, locality, not even upon species! His teaching was the first to emphasize the commonality of all living beings as the basis of relatedness, and was the first to encourage spiritual development that was psychological and social, and that did not rest upon placating some fantasized god. The Buddha realized that liberation lies in our own heart, rather than in aligning with a powerful external Other whom we may be able to cajole or coerce into saving us.

While other religions or cultures had praised virtue, the liberating role of ethics had been previously circumscribed by ritual and by other attempts to manipulate events. The Buddha brought to the attention of humankind the *identity* of virtue and exaltation. His teaching fused into one what had previously seemed like two aspects of existence—empathic ways of living, and gratifying personal feeling states. Through the practice of Vipassana, the Buddha raised into the consciousness of the human community a sunrise of universal, non-tribal, psychological, ethical, non-superstitious relatedness towards all, that advances its practitioner and his or her environment towards becoming vehicles of love and liberty.

Vipassana is not only what the Buddha practiced, but it is what he preached. He encouraged Vipassana practice as universally relevant and beneficent for kings, merchants, housewives and murderers. While he emphasized that not everyone could use Vipassana to become a Buddha within this lifetime, he claimed that everyone could grow on the path. The same sunlight falls on all of us. While we all view different scenes, when we awaken, we all see by the same morning light. Not everyone can benefit to the same *degree* but *everyone* can benefit from the equanimity and loving-kindness that form the foundation of Vipassana.

The uniqueness of Vipassana also rests upon its basis in empiricism. The Buddha discerned the technique by observing what functioned effectively for him. Like any carefully tested observation of nature, Vipassana is a description of natural law that is reliable across time and culture. It is free of antecedent beliefs or assumptions, and contains the same timeless factuality as knowing the ocean is wet and the land is solid. It is more accurately described as an ethical psychology than as a religion. Even to the modern listener, it rings true, not because of ethnoscriptural authority, nor even because of the Buddha's historical apotheosis, but because it harnesses reason and observation to explicate personal experience. It carries us to the edge of the ocean of existence, where our life is bared to realizations that are obvious and inevitable, like the fact that we are temporary visitors in an ancient, ongoing, vast universe.

The definition of Vipassana meditation is: The method by which a person may attain total purification. Total purification means the absence of hate, fear, greed, and delusion, and the presence of love, compassion, and equanimity. Through the practice of Vipassana, a person became the Buddha, that is, he became unshakably anchored in goodness, incapable of harm, and able to explain his methodology to others so that, if their attainments were not as absolute as his, at least their direction would be the same.

Vipassana is merely the careful delineation of common sense. It captures what is common to all civilized communities, and extracts the essence: to avoid harming others, to help others, and to cultivate thoughts and emotions with those same patterns. Even this simple definition encompasses the social, interpersonal, emotional, cognitive, and behavioral development of the individual.

Vipassana is the only path we can take with the conviction that we are following the historical guidance of the most powerful, enduring, and authentic first-person testimonial about personal transformation into absolute goodness.

Unfortunately we are all mammals who identify with the sensations of our own body. We protect them at all costs and often grab immediate palliation and pleasure at the expense of virtues we like to believe we have embraced, but which in fact we place second to continuous self-mollification. We crave pleasure and fear pain. Our journey down the path beyond pleasure and pain can easily be diverted. We need to be grounded in a meditation that roots us in the bigger picture of what ennobles our life. We require a reminder, a discipline, a practice that helps us to draw away from shortsighted reactions to our sensations. We need restorative guidance to activate the life of love and reason in the real texture of our daily adventures. When we anchor ourselves in the perspective of Vipassana meditation, every thought and breath can be incorporated into a path of awareness. Then our smallest choices become the forces that shape our relationship to our body, our emotions, our neighbors and the world. We become travelers of the Path, people who live with conscious intention (though varying success) to activate wisdom in every moment.

Vipassana is unique as the path to total purification, the method of the Buddha, the source of his attainments, the outflow of his realization, and a practical, moment by moment psychology that is ethical, behavioral, emotional, cognitive and spiritual. But "unique" doesn't mean exclusive. Occasionally everyone is spontaneously practicing the same thing: observing how their reactions to little signals of bodily comfort gain too much clout in determining the direction of their lives, and attempting to gain some objective distance from these petty tugs, so that life can flow in harmony with greater and more numinous forces of gratitude, service, and joy. Just as exercise is to some degree intrinsic to human life— though it may be pursued by some people only haphazardly and minimally— Vipassana is the Buddha's term for a natural capacity of our minds. Many people hone it without self-consciously labeling it and many cultures teach aspects of it under different names. All pure beings, regardless of what terms they use, have arrived where they are through detachment from narcissistic preoccupation with the sensations of their own bodies.

All loving, engaged, and generous lives are based upon the same psychological law: practicing equanimity within the sensations of our own life. Vipassana is unique not in the sense that is it better than some other path, but in the sense that it already lies within and flows with any teaching of helpfulness, nonharmfulness, and loving relatedness. Water—the solvent that enables cells, tissues, life—is a compound that is ubiquitous and clear. Rather than rarity, universality makes water unique. Vipassana is unique in its evocation of the general principle. It is unique not in contrast to, but as the active ingredient within all paths of peace. It is not a religion, but a religious psychology; it is not a psychotherapy, though it is psychotherapeutic.

Vipassana simply means clarifying human nature at its junction with the sensations of life. Its uniqueness isn't that it can be found only in an isolated, specialized locale, but that the path to Vipassana begins at every front door.

Because Vipassana commences everywhere, belongs to no one, and has no esoteric teaching nor priesthood to preserve it, it is *itself* only when it is purveyed as common property for the common good. When sold for profit, it is no longer Vipassana— just as physical or emotional intimacy, by definition, cease to be themselves if they are exchanged for money; just as friendship, by definition, has no fee. Vipassana is analogous to a supper among friends who you have invited to your house, while professional psychotherapy is analogous to a restaurant. Vipassana is not comparable to professional healing, which is fairly dispensed for a livelihood by particular healers applying their skills to individual problems in particular ways at particular times and places. If Vipassana is like water, the universal solvent, then professional healing is analogous to medication—an elixir of medicinal use for a specific time, place and person.

2) A Psychological Systems Definition of Vipassana

Vipassana is an ancient, free, nonprofessional, nonsectarian, ethical, universal, psychology of spiritual development. It is based upon methodical, continuous, objective observation of oneself at the level of sensations. This special form of observation catalyzes a multilevel, systems development throughout the strata of one's personality. Part of Vipassana's unique contribution to mental health derives from its *constellation* of psychological actions. Vipassana can be conceptualized as the creation through meditation of a force field that energizes new patterns in six levels of personality.

a) Vipassana induces changes at the *molecular* level of the meditator's body. Systematic, increasingly refined and subtle self-observation, without reaction, alters the flow of stress-related chemicals. The practice of equanimity as a recurrent and lifelong focus, reduces the frequency and intensity with which somatic alarm signals release their neurotransmitters. Storage, release, amount and type of circulating messenger neurochemicals are altered by long term practice of harmony and non-reactivity in the place of anger, fear, or passion. The meditator's body to some degree will, over time, come to consist of different substances than formerly.

b) Vipassana changes the *biology* of the meditator's body. As reaction patterns change, as neurochemical composition changes, and as a self-aware and compassionate lifestyle increases, sleep, diet, and expressions of distress as well as patterns of pleasure may all be affected. Psychosomatic diseases, as well as basic functions like weight, heart-rate, or alertness may be altered. Meditators find themselves choosing to avoid old habits and choosing to cultivate new personal options that spring from a keener relationship to their bodies. If over a lifetime you select a calmer diet and more salubrious relaxations, you become a different animal. Our tissues have the capacity to remold themselves to some extent in response to our friendship with them.

Attunement to our body is automatically experienced as nurturance of it.

c) Vipassana has a dramatic effect at the *psychological* level. Old complexes are relinquished, new attitudes and virtues are cultivated, memories resurface, relationships are seen and developed in new light, the future is deconstructed and reopened in new ways, human history and community are known to have different potentials than was once believed, and event after event in one's life is reexperienced and reexamined in a new perspective. This is the most dramatic and obvious contribution of meditation and the reason it is attractive to many people.

d) Vipassana is value-based education. The goal of Vipassana is to manifest the virtues of love, compassion, joy and equanimity, and as a psychology it can be understood as incorporating direct learning. Virtue is cultivated in privacy, and it is also introjected from the examples of teachers, who may reside as nuclei of inspiration in the minds of their students. In this sense, Vipassana incorporates a *cognitive-behavioral* psychology, that encourages active practice of ideal ways of solving problems, of interacting with others, or of participating in society. Vipassana is also something you *do*. Reverence, respect, gratitude, service are ways to be in the world that can be learned, just like riding a bicycle, and meditation is also a discipleship to right action. Character building is a matter of repetition and effort, not just of sitting still with eyes closed. Vipassana is a training in psychological culture.

e) Vipassana is an *environmental* psychology, that stresses the feedback loop of harmony. The way we treat the world determines much of the response that we will get. This principle is not limited to the human world. The motivations with which we deal with cats, elephants, and trees are also expressions of our psyches, and set in motion responses which we will in turn be receiving back from the recipients of our outgoing messages. For a meditator, respect for life is a logical extension of self-respect. The air, the earth will reply to us and tell us how our wishes, fears and concerns are impacting them and therefore recirculating to us. The world is a sensitive receptor of our inner life. As our inner world expresses itself through actions, the membrane of our surroundings vibrates with the destruction or joy that we have generated. To the meditator, everything around us is a mirror in which we are revealed. Everything around us is also feeling the sting of our wrath, or humming our hum. Awareness of our living environment is the psychological sensibility of Vipassana.

f) Vipassana is a path to *nibbāna,* the transcendence of the material world. Encoded in the psychology of Vipassana is a faith in the More, an intuition of the Beyond. Vipassana is a psychology of the numinous, free from any concrete description, belief, vision, theology, anthropomorphism, fantasy, or reduction of any kind. Vipassana contains an experiential thrust beyond limits of concept and speech, to animating, personality-impacting faith in absolute good.

Vipassana is a unique tool of human growth, transformative from microstructure to illimitable expanse. Nevertheless, it has its proper uses and limits.

3) There Are Limits to Formal Vipassana Courses

Although Vipassana belongs to no one and can be practiced by anyone, anywhere, at any time, formal training courses in Vipassana are not appropriate for everyone at every juncture of their life. To submerge oneself in Vipassana practice all day, every day, for ten days is an intense experience that requires intelligent choice and some discretion as to who should do so, or at what stage of their life. Waiting, choosing the proper time, or forbearing from formal training are all part of the equation of choice.

During long hours of silent meditation, an individual's superficial conscious intentions are unmasked. Beneath our conscious minds are the primitive reactions springing from contact with our body sensations—craving, dissatisfaction, passion, petulance, fear, hate. Can we be at peace with the impersonal ceaseless change of our bodies, that starts at birth and continues to death, and which is the fluid matrix over which we have constructed an image of our apparently stable but truly ephemeral self? The training of a formal ten-day Vipassana retreat is the ability to self-observe our archaic reactions, in the privacy of our own interior life, and to see and to transform who we are at the changing level of guts, bones and heart. Beneath whom we like to imagine we have been, who we really are is clarified and changed. Nothing new is dredged up nor provoked, but who we have always been is highlighted. In the process, our old habit patterns rise up from the unconscious to the surface of our mind. The temptation to act upon old patterns of thought, feeling and behavior is limited by the discipline of the course, as well as by new meditation-derived insights and skills in actualizing who we wish to become.

Formal ten-day courses in Vipassana meditation are built around ethical precepts of behavior, meditative concentration, and the perspective of personal transiency. For all of this to be catalyzed, there are also rules, regulations and time-tables that facilitate an atmosphere in which character strengths are developed and maladaptive reactions released.

There are limits to who can benefit from these formally structured teaching events. People with particular medical problems may find the simple facilities, which are generally designed with modest comfort and the general public in mind, are inadequate for their unique needs. People with some psychiatric problems may also wisely choose to avoid organized Vipassana courses.

The student of such a course must be able to follow rules that ensure the privacy, quiet and proper instruction of all participants. The long days of silence and the detailed guidance require of the student a modicum of trust, cooperation, participation, and earnest effort. People whose psychiatric disorders provoke extreme suspicion, oppositionalism, or apathy clearly will not benefit. Ten days in a drug-free, alcohol-free, smoke-free, celibate environment may also be intolerable to some people.

A more complicated set of situations comes from essentially cooperative, addiction-free people who suffer from overwhelming states of mind, which may vary from intense, garrulous, agitated excitements, to rage, or to distrust, depression, or panic. Here, though there are many variations of possible events, the guidelines are clear: if by character, disease, or temporary state, a person's capacity to follow instructions or to cooperate with a teacher is overwhelmed or subsumed, they will be unable to use formal teaching retreats on the path. If in the past a person has suffered from overwhelming reactions, the technique of silent, days-long self-observation will certainly raise to the surface that same old pattern. Will the new skills in meditative alertness, observation, and insight enable that student to transform their old reactions, or will they once again be subsumed by them? The answer to that lies in the degree and intensity of those past reactions: no matter how severe a feeling may be, as long as attention, participation, working trust, and effort remain intact, Vipassana will provide remarkable power for the student to perceive it, to understand the root of the old reaction, and to find a new avenue of freedom from it.

If, on the other hand, the student knows that in the past their reactions have led to the loss of the constructive and organizing faculties of their personality, then a ten-day Vipassana course is unwise for them. Vipassana courses are not appropriate for the treatment of psychiatric disorders, nor for people with disorganizing mental states. People who require medication to control their emotions should refrain from Vipassana courses until their prescribing physician and they themselves feel confident that they can be both medication-free and able to participate in a course without harming or endangering themselves. There is nothing kind about taking nonswimmers on long canoe trips.

People who can't take ten-day Vipassana courses are still able to benefit from the teaching, but not at the level of intensity provoked by ten days of silence and unbroken awareness of body sensations. Any day, to some degree, old habit patterns of anger, greed, and fear can be relinquished; new growth of tolerance, generosity, honesty, and sobriety can be developed. The practice of all of these beneficent ways of being is itself part of the path. Concentrative meditation, "*ānāpāna*," which focuses only upon breathing, for shorter periods than ten days, is unlikely to stir up deep old reactions, can be relaxing and may be a proper precursor to a ten-day retreat. All considerate words, all grateful memories, may help strengthen the foundation beneath a future of Vipassana practice. Even if a potential student is currently unprepared to face the upwelling of their old reaction patterns, they can still cultivate the character virtues—like gratitude and compassion—that may, over time, provide a containing strength that will eventually enable them to face a meditation course with confidence and success. After such a careful wait and thoughtful anticipation, the old reaction patterns might safely surface to be released during a Vipassana course in the future. The way you live while you wait to take a Vipassana course may be the best possible use of your time, and the wisest strengthening exercise. Some people may benefit from a considered pause before they launch into a ten-day course—a moratorium that may last from months to years—until they gain more confidence that they will be able to endure without cigarettes, or that their old panic attacks or depression have come under more control. Their wait is not an exile from, but a preparation for, a deeper experience.

In the life of a meditator, not all progress can or should be made during meditation retreats. Before and between intensive courses, individuals can employ simple, universal truths to improve their plight and to contribute to society. Having to wait and to work on a problem that would be overwhelming during a meditation course, may itself bring a therapeutic focus to bear upon that problem. It is good to take swimming lessons *before* a canoe trip. The Buddha himself had to search for Vipassana for six years. All valuable tutorials have prerequisites.

Because Vipassana is a natural function of the human psyche—though it was honed and purified and articulated by the Buddha—it has no owner or official institution. Every individual who approaches it is an independent agent whose volition is itself the key to the path. At its core, Vipassana is only the wish and will to cultivate love, compassion, joy, and equanimity. By definition, Vipassana cannot be developed through haste, recklessness, hostility, defiance, or deceit. Its methods and goals are identical.

4) Vipassana Is Not a Psychotherapy

Vipassana is not a psychotherapy because it is not a professionally trained activity, because it is not dispensed as a means of livelihood, because it is not based on a supportive and particularizing relationship with an individual healer, because it is not coadministered with medications or other therapeutic modalities, and because it is not intended as a treatment for psychiatric disorders. But a gray area remains: Vipassana rectifies maladaptive reaction patterns and nurtures character strengths . . . isn't that psychotherapy?

The most important difference between Vipassana and psychotherapy is the place that these two activities are intended to occupy within a person's life. Vipassana and psychotherapy undoubtedly have some overlap in that both are designed to help people live better lives; other than that, they diverge in intention and practice. Psychotherapy is intended as a temporary intervention within the context of a paid, professional relationship, to heal psychological wounds. Vipassana is a free spiritual transmission, a way of life, and a vector beyond life itself. Though it may also bring relief to mundane problems, Vipassana is the path to *nibbāna,* total purification, liberation from suffering. It's time-scale is long—"lifetimes," in the language of the East—and its goals august and embracing. Although our own use of Vipassana in this current lifetime may be much more modest and limited, it still imparts to our lives a momentum beyond our own time and self.

Vipassana is directed towards hope and faith in the future as manifested in this current moment. Its goal is equanimity for oneself now and under all future conditions, and love and compassion for everyone else. It points our vision beyond the temporary horizon. Yet a person may also need an immediate cast upon their broken leg, an acute relief from the terrors of war, or personal help in overcoming past abuse.

A person considering a Vipassana course for the first time would be wise to ask themselves, "What is the intensity of my problem? What is the extent and pervasiveness of my problem throughout the matrix of my personality? What other skills and strengths surround the problem?" Some human dilemmas are powerful but circumscribed. Others are less explosive, yet more pervasive and insidious. There are an infinite variety of permutations of flaws and strengths in each one of us. All of us contain heaps upon heaps of both virtues and negativities, so that our character cannot be measured by a mere handful of either helpful or harmful traits.

Although no schematic, generalized formula can accurately be applied to every case, there are three angles from which scrutiny will be most revealing. Before taking a ten-day course, each person would be well advised to ask of themselves (and the course organizers will want to know): 1) Can I *participate* in rules, regulations, and guidelines that are intrinsic to a guided group experience? If I should develop doubts or mental quarrels with particular instructions, would I be able to discuss them good-naturedly with course managers and teachers, and abide by group guidelines and conclusions about them? 2) The heart of Vipassana is a unique basis for continuous self-observation. Is it probable that I will be able to muster *self-observation* through thick and thin, dawn to dusk, for ten days; or be able to seek help and follow guidance to learn new ways of doing so? 3) Both during Vipassana courses, and in daily life, continuity of effort is the secret of success. Am I mature and steady enough to give a *fair and earnest trial* to Vipassana?

Even if a person is capable of taking a Vipassana course, a certain ambiguity remains as to the proper step for any one person at any one point in time. Rather than this forming an unsolvable problem, the complexity, privacy, uniqueness, and ambiguity of the decision leads to the heart of meditation, which is fundamentally a transformation of motivation. When, why, and how we decide to meditate is itself a part of the practice.

Because every individual is unique, and because at each moment we are different than we had been a moment before, no one else can answer another person's question: "Given these problems that I have, which aren't so severe as to make it obvious that I should avoid a Vipassana course for the time being, should I take an antidepressant, go into psychotherapy, or do you think I would fare better (or worse) if I took a ten-day training in Vipassana?" Remembering the unique contribution of Vipassana, the limits of ten-day courses, and the distinction between Vipassana and psychotherapy, let's look at the way these different behaviors effect individual lives, to highlight the variety of answers that people actually arrive at, and the likely outcome of these varying choices.

5) Examples

The following examples are intended to highlight some of the general principles that I have discussed so far. They are not about the most common experiences that students have on ten-day Vipassana courses, since the majority of meditation students have few conflicts or confusions on these points. The examples are intended to boldly outline the issues at the boundary of Vipassana and mental health, and are fictional composites, which I have divided into three illustrative and somewhat arbitrary groups. Anyone who meditates properly would be a positive example for all three sections. Not so with negative examples. While one person utilizes meditation with understanding, perseverance, and faith, another student who appears similar may use Vipassana erratically or unwisely, leading to problems rather than to solutions.

I) Participation

The application process to a Vipassana course involves honest self scrutiny, as well as feedback from course organizers, but self-deceit or wishful denial occasionally lead a student to commence a ten-day course without the ability to face it.

A heroin addict from suburban New York denied his habit on the application form, and underrated his addiction to cigarettes, so that, from the start, he felt overwhelmed by dual chemical withdrawal. While polite and conversant, he simply refused to stay after the second day, clearly torn by his wish to find a way out of chemical dependencies, and by the power they retained over him, which made stillness and self-observation impossible for him in the face of his urgency and agitation.

A graduate student from the University omitted from his application form his history of delusional thinking and psychotic breaks. He had previously discontinued his medication and his appointments with his psychiatrist based upon his poignant wish for meditation to erase his past. On a Vipassana course, he strove for nearly a week, as he gradually deteriorated. When course managers noted bizarre mannerisms, fasting, and difficulty following the schedule, he was interviewed by the teacher who realized from answers to questions that this student was full of elaborate, self-generated deviations from proper Vipassana practice and was very disturbed, and quietly lost. His family was called, and course organizers and his wife cooperated to restore him to his doctor's care.

These two examples illustrate that meditation retreats aren't helpful to those who start with gross deceit, or who suffer from states of mind that preclude understanding, learning, and practicing as taught.

In contrast, a world-travelling drug abuser withdrew from multiple, hard-drug abuse, and joined a Vipassana course, describing on the application her past troubles and her yearning for a new start. Her honesty alerted the teacher to her possible need for extra help. Her cravings, though powerful, were not too acute for her to observe them using meditation techniques. She completed her meditation course triumphantly. After several months she completed a second ten-day intensive and settled down in a new geographical area for a new shot at life.

Similarly, an engineer described on his application how his college years had been disrupted by mental breakdowns. He had been hospitalized in a psychiatric hospital. Medication and years of psychotherapy had enabled him to earn his degrees, and he had begun his career. When he heard about Vipassana, he was attracted to it as a way to bring more love, compassion, and joy into his somewhat lonely and arid life, but he was wisely cautious about his ability to sit still and observe his reactions! In dialogue with the Vipassana Meditation Center, he began prudent, long-term planning. He continued to work until he had anchored himself in a stable way of life; he solicited his parents' backing; and he reestablished contact with his psychiatrist as a precaution. After several years of good mental health, he successfully started and completed a ten-day course, became an active volunteer at the center, and over a period of many years and many courses, he expanded his social world, opened his heart, contributed to the meditation of thousands of students through his donation of skill and time to the center's physical plant, and he continues to grow on the path.

It is not a diagnostic term, or a single past event, but attitude, understanding, planning, timing, and effort that predict successful use of the Buddha's teaching. Vipassana is not an individualistic withdrawal into self, but participation in an ageless human community.

II) Observation

Completely disingenuous and sincere students may occasionally have to wait or to limit their exposure to Vipassana. This occurs when students carry within them emotions or reactions that erupt unexpectedly and overwhelm them. Despite devotion or commitment, at particular life-stages these students simply will not be able to activate self-observation as the Buddha taught it. To some extent that may be true of all of us! Who would dare to claim the equanimous, objective, self observation of a Buddha? However, among ordinary meditators, some people can persevere in observational effort, while other students, equally solid in almost every other way, cannot, due to the specific organization of the inner life that they bring with them into meditation practice.

For example, a young history teacher and his wife both became students of Vipassana. Delighted by the personal and spiritual results they experienced on their first meditation course, they continued their morning and evenings sittings at home together, took annual ten day courses, and contributed volunteer hours from time to time to the meditation center. They were diligent in maintaining the sober, moral base to their life that the Buddha encouraged, and they found their life increasingly blessed. But things changed. The history teacher's parents died, and he found himself in charge of his mentally ill sister. He was not only burdened with new responsibility, but provoked by memories of his father's drunken abuses that may have contributed to his sister's miserable, marginal existence. As his childhood memories intensified, and as his life became entangled in endless caretaking phone calls to hospitals, government bureaucracies, doctors and police regarding his sister, the history teacher himself became increasingly anxious. He

signed up for another meditation course, hoping to deepen
his capacity for equanimity under his new and tougher life
circumstances, but during the course he was barely able to
observe his sensations, as his mind raced wildly and desper-
ately. Back at home, he continued to persevere in his daily
meditation, but he began to explode into moments of terror that his family practitioner labeled panic attacks. Each
one of these eruptions left him feeling shattered. Despite
his noble efforts to reestablish equanimity in his mind, he
felt he was going to drown in a plight similar to his sister's.
Instead, he sought help at a medical center to which his family practitioner had referred him. For eight months, he
participated in psychotherapy with a psychiatrist, who also
prescribed him medication, and with whom he discussed in
detail his family life, past and present, in order to be better
able to cope with his own memories and with the demands
of his sister's care. During this era of his life, he refrained
from taking meditation courses.

He might have quit meditation at this point. He might
have concluded, "I faced a crisis and meditation was no cure.
Something is wrong either with me or with the technique."
Instead, he stayed in touch with meditation teachers and
friends, avoided judging either himself or Vipassana, and
continued his meditation at home beside his wife as well as
he could. Side by side, they remained confederates of faith
and focus in a vertiginous time.

His morning and evening meditations were now so different, with such powerful mental diversions, such storms
of feeling, so many haunting worries—such a deviation from
the pleasant calm that he had called "meditation" in the past!
His observation now was often limited perforce to his
breath, and even that in a disrupted and fragmentary way.
He might have concluded, "I can't meditate any more. I'm
meditating wrong. My meditation is so bad." Instead, he
had the insight to realize that he had to release his old definition of meditation as a reliably comforting and soothing

relaxation, and to learn to meditate even minimally while snowboarding down an avalanche. His erratic daily meditation did not cure him, but it was helping him far more than he realized, preparing future groundwork for a resilient meditation practice that had many dimensions and could withstand buffeting and travail, and over time gain more dynamic energy to restore equanimity even within acute distress. Meanwhile, he successfully kept in mind the realization: "This awful time, this life-stage, will change, just as my old life did." As his illness responded to psychiatric treatment... he found that he was still a meditator, still bonded to a tradition, still an honest and sane observer of the reality of change in himself. In fact, he was a much deeper meditator than he had been before, because he now had a riveting memory of the reality of change upon change within the structures of what he called himself. The unwanted experience had actually been a stern but useful teaching. What an irony when he found, after completing his psychiatric treatment, that he was now an even more inspired Vipassana student!

No longer fixating on one type of mental experience and labeling it "good meditation," no longer attempting to use meditation as a medical panacea, he understood Vipassana as a window into the universal reality of change, through which he could better face life's storms. Sometimes he might have to seek help, but he would eventually outgrow that plight, while he continued to faithfully glance at ultimate truth through ongoing meditation. His psychiatric treatment had constituted a skillful helpseeking behavior that contributed to longevity as a healthy meditator. For years now, he has required no further treatment; he can cope with his sister, and with himself, with greater balance. He continues to walk the path from which he was never fully disrupted, even when his world seemed detonated.

Continuity of effort to observe was the secret of his success. Vipassana continued to provide insight, meaning,

and direction that surrounded and endured beyond professional medical help. His seemingly catastrophic trial turned
out in retrospect to have been a fiery educational interlude,
while his meditation, which had appeared token and en-
feebled at the time, was in fact a unique bridge from the
Buddha to him, before, during, and after his episode of intense suffering. His taproot in morality, and his realistic
perspective, remained rudders even when his concentration
seemed lost on high seas. When the big waves had at last
faded, his devotion to objective self-observation was still
on course. Psychiatry helped his mental health. The path of
Vipassana moved him along a journey that points towards
helping others, and towards gratitude for help received. With
a long life yet to live, he may well continue his progress
beyond well-being, into helping himself and helping others
realize universal truths while disentangling from parochial
suffering. Vipassana is as deep as the problem it is used to
solve.

There is no wisdom in commencing a first meditation
course while one is overwhelmed and beset beyond one's
ability to cope. A person wracked by agitation, anxiety, depression or doubt cannot expect instant, radical cure in ten
days of flailing and dismay. Vipassana should be allowed to
take root when there is no question that the heart of the
Buddha's teaching—objective observation of the vibratory
basis of the false sense of self—can be comprehended, mo-
bilized, and practiced. Once the path is properly learned,
however, it can be kept alive through the severest trials. In
fact, that is the whole point!

Many students quit meditating when life erupts into
unwanted suffering, or when their concentration deterio-
rates under stress. Many people understandably feel belittled
by the mountains of distress they contain. But there are many
counter examples, of people who spin a thin thread of effort to observe properly even as they tumble down the
mountain. In the long run, it is through this thread that
they feel the belaying power of the Buddha's teaching.

III) Fair and Earnest Trial

Two couples, old friends, came from the east and west coast to take their first Vipassana meditation course together, worked properly, and experienced the exhilarating sense of accomplishment and joy that is so often the fruit of the first deep Vipassana practice. None of them had any particular difficulty participating in the course rules and disciplines, or in continuing to make efforts to return to objective observation of themselves. Each of the four, in the privacy of their own thoughts, was so inspired that they determined to continue the path for the rest of their life. But things did not work out that way.

The woman from California was interested in alternative healing, and she misconstrued the psychosomatic healing power of Vipassana and its bodily attention, as just one more "body-mind therapy." She failed to grasp its uniqueness as a free, universal, ageless, multi-leveled path to *nibbāna*. She mixed it with superficial, tactical, soothing "therapy" workshops and weekends, gradually drifting from meditation, practicing it perfunctorily, and therefore with little gain. She calmed herself with red California burgundy instead of meditating in the evening. As she drifted from one healing fad to another, her anger, irritability, and unhappiness, which had previously impelled her to seek out Vipassana, resurfaced. Augmented by the fantasies of happiness dangled in front of her by the New Age healing marketplace, her negativities oozed further into her daily life and marriage. Gradually, as her depression increased and her relationship with her husband deteriorated, she sought psychiatric help, and was medicated for chronic depression and attention deficit disorder. Incorporating these labels into her sense of self, she quit meditating and accepted the idea that she had biochemical, genetic deficits and would have to remain on medication for the rest of her life.

Her husband became increasingly furious at her self-preoccupation. Proudly, he continued his twice-daily meditation alone, and returned for further ten-day courses. He felt pleased by the pleasant sensations of free-flow in his body as he meditated, and he increasingly looked upon these experiences of ecstatic dissolution as proof that he was holy and attained. Instead of a path of objective observation, he turned Vipassana into a path of sensual self-absorption; instead of a path of compassion, he turned Vipassana into a self-righteous fortress. As he meditated, he indulged in fantasy about his past and future lives, to the detriment of his current one. When his wife finally exhorted him to visit her psychiatrist with her for couples therapy sessions, the husband from California haughtily rejected the psychiatrist's suggestion that he start psychotherapy on his own and take medication to reduce his self-aggrandizing and compensatory delusions.

The couple from California eventually separated. The wife now considered herself a purely medical case, taking psychotropic drugs and dabbling with herbs. The husband became defensively cocksure, and turned his antimedication spurning of psychiatry into a testimony of his spiritual purity. That he was above ever stooping to psychotherapy or medication became the cornerstone of his self-esteem. He pursued an accusatory divorce, bitter, unhappy, and self-justifying. When Vipassana teachers failed to give him the approval he sought for his litigious aggression with its rebirth rationalizations, he quit meditation and threw himself into an "instant enlightenment" group in Los Angeles.

For meditation to be fruitful, there must be reasonable discernment to differentiate the path of a Buddha from trends and fads. Similarly, the use of doctors is optimal when there is a modicum of consumer inquiry. The story of the wife from California illustrates both of these points. Many essentially healthy people end up on medications for predominantly cultural reasons. In a society that encourages consumerism and that conflates health cures with love and meaning, people like this California wife may be diagnosed and medicated for syndromes that stem from overstimulation, subtle and casual intoxication, absence of discipline, and self-absorption. Having failed to find total enlightenment immediately, she grasped haphazardly until she hit the least common denominator that her culture offers. In a different era or culture, where individuals did not feel entitled to a chain of frivolous life choices, her purported attention deficit disorder may have evaporated under a regime of constancy, simplicity, and devotion, and her depression might have melted from the warmth of constructive social contribution and loving family life. As it was, she did not have the knowledge or social guidance to know how to marry a person or a path.

The opposite of quick-fix living is also unproductive. The husband from California was steady but rigid, fanatical but not devoted. He worked long and hard in the wrong direction. He used meditation to feel mighty and aloof, rather than empathic and affiliated. He practiced improperly, setting his own goals and rejecting objectivity and equanimity in favor of bathing himself in pleasurable sensations and escapism. He placed himself above his teachers. Deviating from Vipassana, he engineered a unique contemplative discipline that amplified narcissistic delusion. Ironically, had he listened to his wife's overprescribing psychiatrist he might have nevertheless saved both his marriage and his meditation by at least reducing his delusions. He rejected both psychotherapy and medication not to deepen his capacity to face suffering with noble truths, but to magnify his own ego. In his view, he rejected psychiatry because as a student of the Buddha such mundane help was beneath him—but stubbornness and vanity were even less liberating. Ultimately, he failed to benefit from either psychiatry or Vipassana.

It is instructive to compare this couple to the history teacher. He avoided self labeling of either medical-diagnostic or of "spiritual" varieties; he persevered in right efforts despite difficulty. He clearly differentiated between legitimate medical help and flattering sales pitches, and between the lifetime path of Vipassana and the state-specific psychiatric rectification of psychopharmacology coupled to brief psychotherapy. He differentiated overwhelming necessity from merely convenient or placating misuse of medication; he never poured his pain onto his wife, but sat beside her as a cherished ally; he continued the moral and lifestyle aspects of Vipassana as treasured, self-selected guides that can always be practiced and are always beneficent. Avoiding despair or grasping at facile conclusions, avoiding judgement of his meditation according to the pleasure or turmoil in his body sensations, he walked, maybe staggered, forward, increasingly able to live with compassion for his sister, gratitude towards his wife, and increasing joy and equanimity in himself. Where will his forward motion ever end? What could ever stop such a devoted, even if troubled, practitioner of the Vipassana way?

The east coast friends of the California couple began Vipassana at the same time and with the same steps, but their path was to become quite different. They had an ostensibly more difficult road to travel, yet they *found* the unique contribution of Vipassana to mental health.

The husband had taken birth in a family with a generations long history of poverty and oppression. Exile, terror, and enmity had been part of the atmosphere in which he had grown up, and had permeated his developing nervous system with reactions of fear and despair. Years later he would come to understand that he met the criteria for and could have easily been diagnosed as having depression and anxiety. But after his initial exposure to Vipassana, he put down deep roots into the practice. He determined to use his distress as a continuous catalyst to face reality within himself as objectively and as equanimously as possible. His foray was not mere stoicism. He understood that the path is a way of life, not merely a tactic; he cultivated interpersonal concern and generosity as assiduously as "sitting." He soothed himself with the cleansing calm that accompanies sober, moral lifestyle. He walked forward with the timetable of a lifetime, not with a petulant time limit. Despite and because of his internal memory of deep suffering, he gradually blossomed as a music teacher and a high school chorus conductor. His marriage, suffused from two sides with respect, devotion, and affection, was a source of solace and joy in a life that continued to have its share of raw vulnerabilities. Along with his wife, he actively donated time and energy to make Vipassana more widely available to others. His anxiety/depression was not treated by, but was subsumed under and rotated by Vipassana into a source of determination and direction.

The east coast wife had been psychiatrically incapacitated in her early years. The suicide of her father, its eerie residue, and subsequent deficit in parenting, had left her immature, wanting and expecting other people to take care of her and stalled in the development of adult roles. Unable to constructively engage work or school, she slid into minor drug abuse and dependent sexual misadventures. When she found Vipassana, she worked with it as taught, and almost instantly applied its moral implications to her behavioral disorders, which dramatically disappeared almost overnight. But her growth on the path, like everyone's, was uneven, with some problems more superficial and more easily relinquished, but with others sandblasted into her. Her over-reactive, thin-skinned nature was deeply entrenched. Over many years subsequent to her initial dip into Vipassana practice, she constructed her marriage and her mothering around the Buddha's teaching. Gradually she and her husband built the loving and nurturing home she herself craved and never before had. Every day was a challenge for her to apply the insights which she developed in meditation to her own antithetical predisposition. Her tendency was to react to every minor stress as if it were the death of everything in her world. She had belief in but no familiarity with equanimity. The Vipassana way of life was neither easy nor natural for her, but for that very reason it was more valuable and rectifying, and the more it helped her reduce her fits and compulsions, the more her appreciation for it grew into a deep, well tested devotion. Never facile or saintly, her parenting seasoned from peevishness into balanced caregiving. Her children blossomed into more balanced and capable people than either she or her husband had been. Every day she walked the path, redirecting her life that was easily buffeted but well held. She did not run for therapy or medication to salve every irritation, but built mental muscle by exercising Vipassana against the stress and strain of living. Ironically, those who struggle most to establish Vipassana in their life may be the ones who gain the most from it.

The east coast couple both started life with moderate psychiatric disorders. They did not use Vipassana as a psychotherapy nor as a panacea, nor did it make them perfect or elevate them beyond all distress. But it gave them an efflorescent way of life, redolent with intimacy and appreciation, a home of determination and modesty, which was imbued with the light of the Buddha's love and joy. Their nobly imperfect well-being pulsed outward from them to their children, their friends and community like the earthy scent of spring grass.

The story of the east coast couple is about successful use of Vipassana by ordinary people beset by problems. Both of them were able to *participate* in the guidelines and restraints that enable meditation courses, meditation centers, and functional families. Though haunted initially by anxieties and despairs, they didn't use their personal suffering as rationalizations to disparage themselves, each other, or the disciplines of the path. Understanding the fundamental principles of Vipassana, they cultivated love, peace, and respect for everyone in their home—each other and their children. There was no room for such a heartfelt effort to go awry, based as it was simply on causal logic. When their foibles and passions began to tug them off course, they reactivated *observation* of themselves at the deepest level through devoted meditation at home and in annual retreats. They withdrew from the American national pastime of blame, accusation, and dissatisfaction, and they substituted self-scrutiny of their own contribution to the domestic tensions that briefly flared. Since both of them practiced Vipassana, no one was entitled to assume the role of the righteous accuser; no one was left holding the bag of the pious martyr. The harmony and joy that seeped into their otherwise arduous lives amply justified to them their faith in the path. The east coast couple exemplify the meaning of "a fair and earnest trial." All of this was done without any distinguishing talents and with some nasty blemishes with which to commence. In a society awash in pills, litigation, and fairy-tale cures, they applied the classic, universal truths of insight and gratitude to the roots of their lives, and reaped the only possible harvest of such applications.

As their progress on the path continues, the endpoint of their development remains an ascending unknown. The east coast couple live something different from mere mental health, for they are part of the Path, the continuity of the Buddha's way of life. Briefly, their transient lives form a nodule of peace and rectitude in the tides of time.

Beyond the personal gain that they have gotten, the east coast couple have contributed one star to the sky. Many small vessels in the turbulent waters around them may be steering by their light.

The unique contribution of Vipassana to mental health is neither to fix psychiatric disorders, nor to ignore them, but instead to open individuals to the flow of liberation. Self-observation, equanimity, and sympathetic joy then use these people as conduits to enter and to ease the world. Their individuality, with its particular knots of suffering, unravels, and they align with deeper realities.

Summary

Buddhas are rare. They are so radiant, inspiring and exemplary that they lead millions of people for thousand of years. The further we follow the path they have walked, the closer we will get to the fruits that they have won. But in this lifetime we are likely to lack some strengths and to have many common human frailties. Vipassana meditation blossoms when we have realistic acceptance of ourselves. In every setback, whenever we are knocked down, there is no better time to activate what we have developed so far. Every moment is new, and an opportunity from which we can benefit no matter how long a chain of problems we have yet to solve.

Vipassana is like walking through a series of doors in the house of your own *kamma*. Door after door must be patiently opened, in room after room. Maybe one of these rooms with its slippery marble floors may take you lifetimes to cross. But if you keep going you will at last step out onto the back porch and beyond the house of yourself, beyond all doors at last. Someone may be singing the famous songburst that the Buddha sang at the moment he became fully enlightened, about how he had broken through all walls of himself. It may be you who is singing.

The Experience of Impermanence

By walking down the path of Vipassana meditation, we arrive at experiences that season and mature our personalities. The personal transformation we each undergo becomes the catalyst for social change as we influence everything around us.

The great Vipassana meditation teacher, Sayagyi U Ba Khin, wrote: "Impermanence (*anicca*) is, of course, the essential fact which must be first experienced and understood by practice." *Anicca* is a gateway, an opening.

The complexity and multiplicity of the phenomena of the world can appear like a thicket, but as a person walks the path of Vipassana meditation a clearing emerges. U Ba Khin wrote: "*Anicca* is the first essential factor ... for progress in Vipassana meditation, a student must keep knowing *anicca* as continuously as possible."

The Pāli word *anicca* is translated into English as impermanence or change. But *anicca* is not merely a concept; it is a sign, a marker like the stone cairns a pilgrim encounters on one of those cloud-hugging paths in the Himalayas, signposts to indicate the trail that other true pilgrims have blazed. *Anicca* is a word-indicator that points to a fact of reality: the ceaseless transformation of all material in the universe. Nothing is solid, permanent, immutable. Every "thing" is really an "event." Even a stone is a form of river, and a mountain is only a slow wave. The Buddha said, *sabbe saṅkhārā aniccā*—the entire universe is fluid. For the practitioner of Vipassana, *anicca* is a direct experience of the nature of one's own mind and body, a plunge into universal reality directly within oneself. "Just a look into oneself," U Ba Khin wrote, "and there it is—*anicca*."

For a twentieth-century scientist, *anicca* is an immersion into the factual reality of biology, chemistry, and physics—the atomic and molecular universe—as if, after years of reading cookbooks, one at last could acknowledge that one is the cookie in question.

The experience of *anicca* enables the student of science to feel subjectively what was previously analyzed externally and objectively.

Subjective premonitions of time and change are common to all human experience. We sense *anicca* as we age, and we observe its operations throughout nature.

Polish-born Californian poet, Czeslaw Milosz, a recent Noble Prize winner, returned to rural Lithuania after an absence of fifty-two years, and wrote:

> This place and I, though far away,
> Simultaneously, year after year, were losing leaves.

Shortly after receiving the Nobel Prize for poetry in 1914, Rabindranath Tagore of India analogized the universe to *"balaka,"* ganders on their restless non-stop migration from Siberia to South India:

> …Beneath the veil of earth, sky, water, I hear the
> restless beating of wings.

Four years after Tagore's poem was written, Anglo-Irish poet William Butler Yeats, who was also to become a Nobel Laureate, and who read, admired and helped translate Tagore's poetry, saw time and ceaseless change reflected to him by the wild swans at Coole:

> But now they drift on the steel water,
> Mysterious, beautiful;
> Among what rushes will they build,
> By what lake's edge or pool
> Delight men's eyes when I awake some day
> To find they have flown away?

If *anicca* is so pervasively intuited and scientifically factual, why do we have to work so hard to know it? Isn't it obvious, everywhere, to everyone, all day?

Our resistance to the experience of *anicca* is the great sorrow: *sabbe saṅkhārā dukkhā*—all things are filled with suffering. We maintain direct experience of *anicca* at arms length, as a scientific concept or a poetic sentiment, because its dynamism melts our sense of security and order, and fills us with a sense of loss and sorrow.

Everyone likes the idea of being purified by a dip in the Ganges, but to anyone standing on its banks as it emerges from the mountains at Rishikesh or Hardwar, icy cold and with a dangerous current, there has to be a moment of hesitation, if not outright retreat, before the actual plunge. And so much more with a river that won't purify you unless it washes you away. A dip into *anicca* clarifies reality, but it pulls us away from the comfortable, known shore, and that tearing away is initially frightening and painful. The great sorrow, dukkha, leads to the loss of comforting myth, familiar alliance, and secure identity—all the hooks by which we cling to the idea that we have an eternal, immutable, personal self that will never be washed away from us into the river of life. And so we realize, *sabbe dhammā anattā*—all phenomena are insubstantial. The fantasy of our own greatness, the love we have for ourselves and everything we call ours, is the rock on which all of us build our lives. But every rock is a form of river. Even, or especially, the rock of the self is revealed to be liquid, essenceless, *anattā*. How terribly, terribly sad it is to feel our lives slipping down the relentless, cold current of time. Not a scripture in the world is free of this outcry of sorrow and disbelief that the minds and hearts and homes and families we cherish will all be stripped away from us on our passage across this earth.

The psalmist wrote:

> Thou turnest man to destruction; and sayest,
> Return, ye children of men.
> For a thousand years in thy sight are but as yesterday
> when it is past, and as a watch in the night.
> Thou carriest them away as with a flood....
> (The Bible, Psalm 90)

In the great epiphany of the Bhagavad Gita, Chapter XI, we read of "all-powerful Time which destroys all things," which is portrayed as a world-consuming conflagration, a fiery finale to all hopes and dreams.

The Koran, *sura* LVI, reminds us of a time "When the Terror descends ... when the earth shall be rocked and the mountains crumbled and become a dust scattered ...." It is up to us to understand that that day is every day.

II

With his characteristic straightforwardness, courage, and clarity, Freud dared to shock his readers with his views on organized religion. He wrote that every member of human-kind felt small and helpless against the forces of nature, preeminently death. The thought of death wounded the individual's sense of narcissism. Freud felt that every indi-vidual was to a greater or lesser extent like Narcissus, the Greek mythic figure who fell in love with his own reflec-tion. To heal the wounds inflicted by awareness of time and death upon each of our own narcissistic feelings, Freud said, humans bond together in collective narcissistic excitement. Thus we see collectives like nation-states or organized reli-gions join in self-proclaimed self-importance. This herd drama helps the individual to feel that even though his own beautiful self may fade and die, at least he is part of some-thing enduring, important, and powerful. We need only remember when Freud was writing to realize how tragically keen his insight was; soon all of Europe was to explode into hordes of self-aggrandizing murderers who justified their actions on transcendental grounds: I am part of the father-land, I am forging human history. Heinrich Himmler, who was in charge of the S.S., the special forces whose job was to kill innocent noncombatant Jews, told his men that he knew they sometimes suffered confusion and guilt over what they were doing, but they should not be deterred, for they were serving their Leader and Fatherland in "an unwritten and never-to-be-forgotten glory."

Freud's psychoanalytical psychology clarifies the link that joins falling in love with an image of one's own idealized, beautiful self—narcissism—with the narcissistic injury that no person can avoid when even a glimmer of death crosses his mind; and both to the final link in this small chain: the psychological defense against death provided by group narcissistic inflation. Grandiosity—overweening self-importance—whether individualistic or collective, is one way that small people can experience themselves as safe and powerful. Grandiosity is a common security operation in a world of insecurity. As Freud so poignantly foresaw, the greater the insecurity of the times, the greater the likelihood that people will huddle into defensive, self-protective, self-trumpeting clusters. The power of these human whirlwinds is as great as the terror that underlies them. They are inaccessible to reason because they spring not from ideation or dogmas (which are secondarily used to justify and rationalize them), but from deeper psychological strata: the egoistic desire to transform the world into a stage for one's own, indelible self. From a desire for permanence to narcissism to grandiosity to social aggression: mob membership is a common reaction against the great sorrow that is immanent in human life. Intelligence and culture are no palliative: the greatest Western philosopher since Plato, Martin Heidegger, publicly espoused Nazism. Similarly, exhortation to abstract values like compassion and service can be used to fuel the fire of self-importance. When Nathuram Godse assassinated Mahatma Gandhi, he justified his behavior as an act of selfless courage in the service of his motherland. But his own words in his defense revealed his fear of being weak, "emasculated" and vulnerable.

Henry David Thoreau was probably the first American to have contact with, and attempt to practice, India's ancient pathways to wisdom. He wrote, "Most of what my neighbors consider to be good, I consider in my heart to be evil; and if I repent of anything at all, it is of my good behavior." It is in the name of the gods, and the groups, that most murders are done in the service of the chimera of greatness. From the crusades to the ongoing religions and ideological warfare on our planet today, we can see activation of the link between the human ability to imagine personal death, and the reactive, outraged denial of such frailty, with the result of power-seeking and violence. Rather than correcting this disease of the psyche, organized religions often provide a channel, similar to politics, through which the howl of incredulous despair can strike out.

III

Sabbe saṅkhārā aniccā. The individualistic drive to transform the world in accordance with egoistic desires underlies social rage. Vipassana counters that drive at its root. So far I have been discussing the experience of *anicca*; now I want to stress the **experience** of *anicca*. One insight Freud shared with the Buddha is that by **directly** confronting the source of our suffering, we can be freed. To be human is to suffer; to be fully human is to suffer consciously. Vipassana meditation enables the ordinary individual to see what is hidden, to confront the elusive, to envision the unimaginable. Change is invisible; reality is elusive; the evaporation of ourselves is unimaginable to most of us most of the time. Yet through a gradual, guided, time-tested process, we may grow in our human capacities. Vipassana provides a developmental ladder by which we can continue to climb upwards, just as we did as toddlers when we learned to walk, or as we did as schoolchildren when we learned to read and write. What is terrifying and impossible when viewed as a whole becomes challenging and possible when viewed step by step.

The rung of the developmental ladder where we now stand is the experience of what might be called *anicca*-in-spite-of-ourselves. Because there is a great resistance in our hearts to *anicca*, because of the great sorrow involved in the loss of our image of ourselves—with which we have narcissistically fallen in love, and which we want to preserve and defend by the exercise of willful power—because we each seek security and satisfaction in life through an aggrandized, projected sense of the idealized self as we imagine it to be forever, the experience of *anicca* comes with pain.

Is there a Vipassana student who never got up at the end of a determined sitting without at least two small channels of the river of life flowing down his or her face?

Anicca is what we run from; *anicca* is what we fear; *anicca* is what we join forces against and attempt to smash. *Anicca* is the destruction of our personal power, the loss of our world as we know it. *Anicca* is what drives the world mad. But the **experience** of *anicca*, a precious and fortunate opportunity into which one develops slowly—it is said, over lifetimes—the actual direct experience, as opposed to our images, bugaboos, and sideways glances—the experience of *anicca* is a simple, clear, fact, like the wind.

It is a release, like a dip in a healing, cool, fresh river. Now I am washed away in the river; after so much fussing, I am torn away and alone in the current. But I can swim, or rather, float. The self I held, I left with my towel on the shore, but I'm still alive; I haven't drowned or died. Pieces of what I imagined I had to grip to me come floating along beside me. The current of the world is unraveling in faces and forms. Without my will the universe unrolls, and fills my arms with muscles, my heart with human concerns. The scintillating milky way of my back is a winking and shimmering constellation; my body itself is a river, a continent of rivers, a flickering, vibrating, shoreless ocean of currents and channels, unfathomable, beginningless, endless. The living ride on life like foam on the crest of a surge in the cosmic ocean.

The experience of *anicca* leaves one floating on the exfoliating, impersonal truth, the ocean of life. The flood of life need not drown us; it can instead buoy us up if we learn how to swim. The experience of *anicca* is the place to plunge in and be turned into a fish, a wave, a fleck of foam on the surging expanse of life itself.

The three Nobel-Prize winning poets who I quoted in the beginning of this essay all deepened in their ability to absorb the painful truth. Czeslaw Milosz, who felt himself "losing leaves", found intact an old meadow of his childhood and, "Suddenly I felt I was disappearing and weeping with joy."

Aging, sick, near death, Tagore felt his body floating down an ink-black stream,

> ...as shadow, as particles, my body
> Fused with endless night. I came to rest.

Yeats wanted his last words to champion detachment, and gave this directive:

> In Drumcliff churchyard Yeats is laid...
> No marble, no conventional phrase;
> On limestone quarried near the spot
> By his command these words are cut:
>> Cast a cold eye
>> On life, on death.
>> Horseman, pass by!"

The experience of *anicca* is not the endpoint of the path of Vipassana. It is not *nibbāna*, the transcending of the transitory world of mind-and-matter. It is not the final goal of enlightenment. But it is itself a critical step on the path toward that goal, and liberating in important ways. The path of Vipassana, as taught by the Buddha, leads away from craving and aversion that derive from a rigid self-concept, away from negativities of greed, hate, and delusion that derive from defense of the false, ephemeral self. The path opens into the virtues and qualities produced by experienced insight. The realization of *anicca* is a deep insight into ourselves and the world around us. It exposes the absurdity of clinging to a passing life in a passing world. It relaxes the clenched, false hopes of narcissism, and enables the flow of spontaneous identification with all other transient lives. From the experiential realization that all things are *anicca*, that I am *anicca*, comes the deepest empathy possible: a feeling of kinship with all beings who suffer alike from the pain aroused by the illusion of separate self; a feeling of fellowship with all beings who yearn for liberation from the agony of separation, dissolution, death.

IV

The loss of self in the experience of *anicca* is not a rejection of mundane obligations, a flight from interpersonal responsibility, nor a loss of ordinary, functional life-skills. It is a perspective that embraces and validates these aspects of routine existence, but places them in proportional importance within a comprehensive context, the way that farms seen from a New England mountaintop become even more beautiful, though clearly only islands of cultivation surrounded by more extensive, shadowy woodlands.

There is nothing in the experience of *anicca* to make a person abandon the immediate contingencies of his or her social, familiar, or professional existence, for the experience is neither a excitement nor an intoxication.

The practice of Vipassana meditation leads to activation of the experience of *anicca*, which in turn leads to a maturation, not an eradication, of personality. The life I thought I was living I now know is living me, and I've got work to do. Not "my" work, but work. Laid out in front of me and around me are the events with which I am ceaselessly, inevitably interacting. I can be called, but not by the tin drum of grandiosity. I do belong, but not to a mob. I walk, but don't march. When asked, I point out to others those pagodas on a hill—where I sit down to focus on the experience of *anicca* as it manifests on the field of my mind and body—those buildings that took so much time and energy to build, and which stand like a cairn on the otherwise trackless mountain of life, but which I know will blow down in one storm or another, only to sprout up again on other mountains, among other travelers. I point out that meditation center on the hill as a good place to have a seasoning, sobering experience.

Vipassana leads to a slow, cumulative social change by organizing individual lives around new sources of well-being. It points to a sense of aliveness that is marked by a tenacious steady investment in the personal and the real. It weakens the call of the trumpet, and evokes the music of the wind and rain. It makes pain more bearable than hate. It makes equanimity sweeter than excitement. It makes death more welcome than conquest. It makes service nobler than heroism. It makes sorrow and joy run back and forth into each other like twin rivulets intersecting, entwining, and separating again on the same hillside. It leads to an equipoise beyond the poles of pleasure and pain.

The experience of *anicca* leaves no way out but the path—for the entire phenomenal world is *anicca*. There can be no hope for the ambitions of the individual, despite all his narcissism and grandiosity. Yet there can be hope. As the raindrop descends, does it know its body will be absorbed by the roots of grass or trees, to be consumed by animals, to flow into milk, one day at last to dance in the blood of a singing child? All is *anicca*; mind and body helplessly flow in impersonal becoming. In spite of this current, a movement is possible towards liberation from ignorance and towards attainment of insight. Realization of *anicca* catalyzes further bodily discipline and mental insight, so that both mind and body are accelerated towards their own transcendence. As the raindrop cycles through grass, animal, milk, and child, it moves from a state of inert physicality to participation in hopeful human possibility. The elements cooperate when orchestrated by the wisdom of the path. Striving to know *anicca*, meeting and immersing in *anicca*, people can turn the world toward liberation.

Generosity, compassion, simplicity are the spontaneous expressions of a world view in which nothing can be kept, suffering is a common bond, and materiality is only an obstacle to a finer trajectory of spirit. People who have vibrated deeply in *anicca* know that every pocket sooner or later gets a hole. Since nothing can be kept it might as well be shared.

The experience of *anicca* through the process of Vipassana meditation leads to the transformation of narcissism and grandiosity into mature participation, service, love. It reveals individualistic life to be a sieve. It breaks open a stone to reveal a star.

V

The kernel of the path is so simple it can be explained in one sentence: transcend the suffering involved in attachment to the self—mind, body, and the world associated with them—by observing objectively and peacefully the arising and vanishing of everything composing them, thereby cultivating insight into their essential transience. In my own experience, I find I wander away from and back to this core truth a million times. There are many lives I have to live, many fears I have to overcome, many growing hands I have to guide, many companions I have to meet, and many as yet undiscovered lakes that call to me from their hidden recesses in the wilderness to come and watch their animals and breathe their mists, before I will be able to sit down and fix unwaveringly and finally upon *anicca*. I have much to learn about this truth, but every moment of acquaintance with it grips me in an unalterable turning.

1989

Touchdown *Anicca:* An Evocation of Meditation in Everyday Life

Between formal Vipassana practice and the general guidelines for living which the Buddha taught, lies the moment by moment experience of the person who is careening through their intricate, annoying, frustrating and triumphant workaday life.

I want to write an evocation of the use of meditation outside of formal retreats, in the maelstrom of daily life. I want to capture the texture of a devoted meditator's routine hours, praising the contribution that Vipassana can make to a life within the confines of the hands of clocks, the sludge of paperwork, the rhythms of school-day breakfasts, the puncture of telephone answering machines firing their salvos, the tingle of tea and trusted talk. These repetitive chores and habits consume most of our earthly existence. How can one live Vipassana moment to moment, day to day?

Vipassana meditation is the nexus of a way of life that is framed by seated, still, and silent meditation on the one side, and by rules for the good life. Between these two is a descriptive gap, within which lies a realm of increasing significance to the type of student who is learning Vipassana today, who wants to practice in a contemporary, lay context.

But what does *practice* mean when I am filling out insurance forms, mowing a lawn, or discussing arithmetic homework with a child, and my eyes are open, my body is in motion, and my mind is focused on completing tasks? In the essay, *The Experience of Impermanence*, I defined *anicca*, and discussed its profound depth and revolutionary implications. An immersion in the experience of *anicca* is possible through prolonged Vipassana meditation retreats. But what good is such a deep spiritual dunking when I have to return to a world of income taxes, neighbors' dogs trespassing and attacking me, and aging parents?

The goal of a lay meditator in the modern world is to develop his or her access to the experience of *anicca* so assiduously that a channel to it is permanently open. With this availability of deep experience well established, through annual Vipassana courses and twice daily sitting, one can live the Buddha's timeless path even while one is being swept forward on the conveyor belt of post-technological chronology. This is a life within an eternal now that includes a digital wristwatch.

A metaphor for meditation in the active zone is "touchdown *anicca*."

In colloquial American English, the word *touchdown* has two different meanings. First, it is a football term, the goal of the game—a touchdown is when a player carries the ball across the zero yard line into the end zone. He scores, and the crowd goes wild.

Touchdown is also a traveler's term—the jet roars off the runway and flies until touchdown on the tarmac at the airport of destination. For the broken, hijacked, or endangered jet, touchdown remains the goal, the moment of safety.

For the established, serious and devoted meditator who is nevertheless embroiled in family and professional life, *anicca* is the touchdown. You can't play the whole game there; you can't get there without first taking off and leaving safe ground; but *anicca* is the goal of the game, the destination, the moment of safety.

Anicca can be present increasingly continuously without withdrawal into formal meditation. For almost all Vipassana students today, life is a far cry from the idealized world of meditators of old, who, we imagine, lived without labor in leafy tropics, where no fax, e-mail, phone call or snail mail insinuated itself under the skin of their gracious ease, and where food was presented as a gift, and no shelter was needed but the benign blue sky. Our society requires mastery of anxiety and stress during high speed, high complexity, interpersonally intense tasks. A meditator's life is necessarily a flight away from, but then, from time to time, a touchdown in *anicca*. We are always carrying the ball between tacklers towards the end zone of *anicca*.

II

Let's take a look at a meditator, running along on the field of modern life, encountering its obstacles, and in turn provoked into his own reactions.

He is at work, a job he fundamentally enjoys, that helps people, but which has its own stresses, with which he has learned to cope. Today, however, he is struck out of the blue by deeply unsettling news: the organization for which he works has signed large new contracts calling for *increased efficiency*, which he knows is a euphemism for firing staff to decrease costs. Multi-million dollar financial wheeling and dealing tower and sway around him, and he recognizes his own job to be a precarious, insignificant footnote to cold international finance. He might get fired!

Financial terrors spring up like serpents inside him, weaving and bobbing with chilling power in his mind. One fear raises others in linkage. His mind is flooded with life's bad outcomes, and his body becomes sweaty and cold. He thinks:

"The economy is undergoing a major transformation and my job is at risk. If I lose my job I'll lose my house. My children will be traumatized. I'm too old to learn a new job with its own stresses and complications. I'll be fired again and become distraught. How would I be able to sleep under such repetitive distress? I'll be driven overboard. My entire life is at stake, based on these uncontrollable economic trends, and there's nothing I can do to protect myself, since these events are based on international macroeconomics, global issues. No manager in this impersonal market will care about my fate. What can I do; where can I turn?"

As this fear sweeps through his mind and body, he reaches out, in a well-learned mental gesture, to touch the experience of *anicca*, if only for a moment, seated in his swivel office chair. The experience is direct, sensation based, and deeper than mere thought, a preverbal experience; but to write about it, I can only describe its subsequent verbal residue. He experiences *anicca*, and as he does so, his mental pattern changes, from fear and conviction, to perspective and possibility.

For a moment he meditates with eyes closed, *anicca*, felt initially only in palms, soon becomes reality also in forehead and paraspinal muscles—*anicca* rising like dawn into his mind—and he realizes and begins to understand all these sensations are composed of millions of atomic, flickering changes. "This whole body (not *my* body) is flowing, motile, transient; soon its entire life will be past, and all its ideation, including these economic fears, will evaporate into cosmic time, like the trembling of a mouse, or the crawling of an ant on its hill. The future I so definitively and fearfully foresee in my mind will not unravel as I imagine it, for it is really uncertain, unknown, fluctuant and dynamic, filled with many possibilities I can't foretell now as I sit here. I will have many options, trials, openings and actions unveiled to me as my life unfurls, and my feelings and perceptions will change, as will my mood, over and over, as I roll forward into time; and amidst all this ephemeral uncertainty the one thing I really can say I know is that right now, at this moment, my fears are the temporary excrescents of this vibrating, changing impermanent body ... and are themselves inaccurate forecasts, illusion. Right now, I feel—I know—*anicca, anicca* throughout my mind and body, nothing but flow that isn't me, a changing present, a changing future, that is easy to watch, easy to detach from; and right now, I feel a growing peace, which I know I can return to, through meditation, again and again, as my days emerge in time. I am, and can be, free, within the context of arduous and challenging changes."

Our economically threatened meditator returns to his job calm and uncalmed, clutched and released, ignorant and wise. He takes a few more moments during this memorably unsettling day to touchdown on *anicca*, and, when he returns home, after explaining this new contingency to his wife, and after supper, and after attention to homework and children's bedtimes, they meditate together for an hour. His fears rise and take off like jet planes, and he struggles to touchdown on *anicca*. This practice, this effort, last for weeks, as his uncertain economic future unravels. For him, this bruising affront to the smooth flow of his days becomes an opportunity to deepen his perspective again and again, to both solve and face his job problems while holding them in the context of a realistic perspective, as provided by the experience of *anicca*. His ability to touchdown in *anicca* grows; the depth of his experience of *anicca* grows; anxiety he carried inside him, long before this particular series of events, surfaces repeatedly, and, with the wisdom that rises up from the experience of *anicca*, he releases the top layer of anxiety serially, so that the size of his stack of anxieties is actually decreased, rather than increased, by the turmoil he faces. Instead of the counsels of fear, he has come in contact with a great old teacher of courage.

III

Possibly there are people whose realization of *anicca* is so unshakable that their consciousness never deviates from it. Such an enlightened person would live suffused by wisdom without delusion. The metaphor of a touchdown wouldn't apply to this person, who would be more like the earth, always and only its verdurous self.

But for most of us, daily life is an alternation of mundane reactions, that scatter upwards from our mind when the wind of trouble touches us. Our thoughts wheel and flutter in disarray, until we touch back down to the realistic perspective *anicca*, which, though deeper than thought, also changes our thought, and brings it back down to earth.

Until a meditator becomes fully enlightened, he or she remains a patchwork of ignorance and wisdom, a quilt still being stitched.

When I have listened to the dialogue of ignorance and wisdom in my own mind, it has at times sounded like a parliamentary debate within the kingdom of my *kamma*. A leading spokesman for immediate, self-serving impulse leaps to his feet, and declaims clamorously the virtues of gratification, now! A representative of the wisdom that springs from experiences of *anicca* then takes the floor, speaks movingly and convincingly for delaying action until the whole perspective has been grasped. His measured voice is quickly drowned out as misguided personal patriots shove him aside and deliver impassioned diatribes about taking care of Mr. Number One. When the *anicca* reps regain the mike, they calmly explain the virtues of patience and compassion, but the misanthropes and chauvinists are busy whipping up rhetoric for battleships, guns, or even for strategic retreat followed by guerilla war!

Over the years I have heard the deep voice that represents *anicca* growing in parliamentary stature, while the vociferous nationalists and isolationists have gradually, despite their attention-grabbing bluster, been discredited by their quickly outmoded, situational positions, and by the ill-ease and turmoil engendered by their very tone of voice. You can't build a happy state through tumult and divisiveness. Slowly *anicca*'s ameliorating and reliable program has eroded the reactive protectionists, until their squabbling is diminished throughout the land of mind-and-body. The voices from *anicca* not only refute the harangues of ignorance in the mind, but the militarization of the body as well.

Meditation is not an ideology, but no thinking person has their thoughts untouched by its resonance. The deepest wisdom is felt, realized; but in the politics of the mind, an equable and affiliative utilitarianism that has formed a co-operative government with the representatives of timelessness, produces an unbeatable governance. Right thoughts are those which on a daily basis increase peace and compassion in the psychic economy.

IV

Ignorant reactions take many forms, and may reassert themselves as passions. Let us take a look at a meditator struggling with this problem.

As she turns the corner on forty or fifty years, a seismic tremor rises up inside of her, a reaction that says: "My life has been so beautiful; I can't bear the thought of losing it. The body is so full of pleasure. Look at that young man over there, so strong, so well built, so excited by his partner's presence, what joys and pleasures they will share while I age, wrinkle, gray, pass on, lost to youth, lost to the adventure of new locations, the romance of attention turning towards me with signaled but unspoken desire—how can it be that I will have to part with health, strength, the robust activities by which I defined myself among my friends; how can I live without passion's animating expectations? I can't bear this!" But this meditator is devoted to the practice, and, twice daily and in-between she touches down on *anicca*, and her mental life matures.

Like an ocean tide washing up onto the beach, while meditating, while attending to sensations for a few moments before sleep, *anicca* rises up into body and mind, lapping at the perimeters of craving and ill-ease, *anicca*, *anicca*. Her experience is highly subjective and difficult to describe but after it, she finds herself thinking: "This body is as impermanent as the seasons. The years of my past once seemed so real and now are so lost, so gone, like the sensations in the body I carry already changed from a moment ago. Clearly the only harbor of safety is detachment from this illusory self, from this body-bound life. Yet joy is real; beyond the fading pleasures of my senses are the divine dwellings of peace and love whose wavelengths circle the globe. Love that doesn't clutch can cross galaxies, connect life to life across the vacuums of eternity, the way that the compassion of a Buddha pervades the atmosphere for thousands of years after his death and reaches me. So my own love for other beings may spread out and touch others, a real love beyond body, based on transcendence of attachment to body, which I can attain only by concentrating right now on sensations while realizing *anicca*. This temporary, minute, sub-tingling, flowing down my torso and arms at this moment ... is *anicca*. Awareness of this diminishes passionate craving."

Return to the reality of *anicca* dissolves passion the way that ocean waves smooth beach pebbles, slowly, over a long time, rounding away jagged angles. In reality, the world is always awash in tides of change.

Our aging meditator may gradually relinquish the significance of the bodily pleasures as central to her life. Instead, as she experiences *anicca* more often and more deeply, her thoughts may turn from envy of youth to sympathetic joy in the well-being and accomplishments of others. Now her fading passion appears more like an opportunity to commit more energy to helping other people find the peace of meditation. Rather than frustrations, her losses produce openings—opportunities to deepen her wisdom and expand her service. She observes the growth of young friends with quiet pleasure.

V

What does the experience of *anicca*, with its attendant detachment and perspective, do to family relationships? How does an apparently cosmic concept like *kamma* actually influence the texture of a mundane household day? Let's take a look at a meditator at home.

Her daughter is talking to her, but her tendency is to ignore the child. A busy parent is under constant pressure. When both parents work, do household chores, and parent, no one has a moment to spare. Completion of daily tasks may take precedence over emotional tone. Parents are pushed by time limitations to get the shopping done, to pay the telephone-electric-mortgage-gas-online-service bills, to re-register the car and repair the sliding door. This meditator-mother, into whose fictional existence we are peering, feels behind the schedule. She has yet to do the laundry; she'll have to get dinner on the table, and she hasn't even started to prepare for her work the next morning. She thinks to herself:

"This child is exhausting! What does she expect from me? Can't she see how busy I am? I know she's bright, but her prattle is childish. I haven't got time for that. Why can't she amuse herself? What's wrong with her? Children today are so outrageously demanding!"

But this mother is also a Vipassana meditator, and almost automatically, as her state of annoyance escalates, she begins to observe it at the level of sensations. At the back of her neck she feels her hair prickling as if she were a she-wolf on the defense. Across the top of her back, a hot cord lassoes and tugs at her trapezius muscle. Irritable tinglings descend the biceps of her arms and agitate her forearms and palms. This silent and internal riot by the riffraff of her mind makes her burst out laughing. "Why am I doing this to myself? Is this the right way for me to live?" Her observation once again plays across the surfaces and depths of her body as she stands in her kitchen suspended halfway between filling the washing machine with stained jeans and listening to her daughter describe her friend's dolls. This happens swiftly, a moment of concentration, observation, the sensations of her neck, shoulders, arms already radically altered from a second before, soft running of dots washing away tensions, and the realization of *anicca* arises in her mind and then passes. The direct experience of *anicca* is fleeting. It is already gone. But the mother's thoughts have taken a new turn in response to the experience, the way that a harried messenger in the night may pause and be renewed by the first rays of dawn. She thinks:

"This is the moment; this is reality; this is my life, just a chain of moments passing like beads on a cosmic rosary. I may never get to hear these same words said in the same way again. My daughter is growing, changing moment by moment, never quite who she was the day before, a ceaselessly new mystery under my care. Her silly doll-talk is an inquiry. She is trying to understand relationships, how to get along with friends, how to solve differences, as their dolls hug and fight. The manner in which I attend to her right now may confirm the validity of her earnestness. A few words of proper guidance may help her. Who knows if such a moment will come again? At this moment (vibrating sensations in my head, wires releasing in my feet) I have, as a mother, the power to evoke more love and intelligence into the world, by bringing the fullness of my attention to bear on this conversation. Stained jeans can wait!"

She says, "Yes, dear, tell me more about why the dolls were angry…"

In any moment love and peace can flow from person to person, eternal truths in a transient world. Touchdown on *anicca* can siphon a proper priority up from the clutter. Loving kindness is like gravity, holding together two heavenly bodies.

Of course this moment can't last. *Anicca*. Our fictional Vipassana mother can listen and love, but she also has to get some things done. On to cooking supper (the jeans will have to wait until Saturday). Unfortunately, just as some hot soy oil splatters out of the big black iron frying pan, her husband appears, and wants to know what happened to check number 5499, which she failed to record in the check register. She thinks:

"Why is he pestering me? Can't he see I'm busy? Doesn't he realize I'm behind? Does he want to eat, or go hungry? He is just like a child! Men are so needy. He demands my attention like a four year old. Where are his manners? It's his mother's fault ... the way she raised him! Hasn't he learned *anything* through all these years of our Vipassana practice together?" She has barely enough where-withal to muster up awareness of sensations.

Our Vipassana mother, who is a busy professional dur-ing the week as well, has nevertheless focused her life successfully enough over many years to have taken a dozen ten day courses in Vipassana, several longer courses, and has meditated twice daily thousands of times. Therefore, in the welter of demands upon her, she still remembers to ob-serve the bodily basis of her irritation with her husband. She feels the gross tightness in the slabs of her back, her rapid heartbeat, her short-fast breath, and beneath them all, the subtly flowing atomic transformations within the ag-gregation of material called "body." She has touched down on *anicca*. She realizes change, pervasive impersonal change, throughout herself, throughout all mind and matter, an end-less flow of worlds upon worlds through time and space, within which her body/mind is a brief, insubstantial appari-tion. Two seconds ago she was dodging the hot splattering oil and ready to burst out: "Get lost! I'm cooking! Can't you see that? What's wrong with you? Get out of here!"

But now, as the direct, wordless experience of *anicca* fades, she finds herself musing inwardly: "Across from me right now is another being, my husband, who has been the center of my companionship and support, who has devoted his own fleeting life to the mutual care of our family. His body and mind are impersonal cosmic dust, atoms of earth. Yet we have shared compassion and joy. Will such a friend, will such a sacred partnership ever emerge again in world after world for me? Why not use this moment to express my gratitude for his friendship and encouragement on the path?"

Can you believe that recurrent touchdown on *anicca* changes not only subsequent thought content, but tone of voice as well? There are many ways to say, many sub-texts

implied, in a few simple sentences like, "I'm busy right now.
I promise to look into that right after supper."

"And oh, by the way, I was just fantasizing about telling
you—so now I am—about what a wonderful partner you've
been for me, from our confused and unformed youth, hitch-
hiking through Europe, to our domestic temple of mutual
reverence and respect, right now. Thank you."

Harmony is a flowering plant with leaves in the kitchen
and roots that reach way down deep into *anicca*.

VI

Due to the fact that the words composing this essay are
symbols, the evocations of the experience of *anicca* described
here may be misleading. A reader without personal experience of *anicca* may imagine that I am describing simply one
possibility among many equally valid mental tactics to block
impulsive action, or to correct pessimistic cognitive distor-
tions, or to delay and broaden situational assessments. In
this misperception, I seem to be describing a fragment of
behavior therapy, a kernel of cognitive therapy, a spin-off of
intellectual analysis.

The **experience** of *anicca* is more like the moment in
which the girl from Iowa stands on the beach at Cape Cod
and surveys the Atlantic; or the boy from New Jersey first
sees the snow-capped peaks of the Colorado Rockies. A
new vision of reality forms in an instant. The world-view of
the past permanently shatters. A new truth is grasped ef-
fortlessly—not grasped, but absorbed, inhaled. "I will never
forget the moment that I first looked out across the ocean
and saw no land, no place, just open sky and sea yawning
out in front of me." This sort of pause is not a hesitation or
a reassessment, but a crossing of a threshold into a new being. The **experience** of *anicca* is the realization of
essencelessness and change throughout the material world.
Still, the experience may be more or less deep, more or less
internalized, analogous to the way in which two mid-
westerners may survey the surf pounding the Wellfleet dunes,

and one quickly runs back to the car to escape the wind and salt spray, but the other gazes transfixed and unmoving. The experience of *anicca*, with each exposure, "takes" more and more deeply.

When *anicca* is understood as an intellectual ideology divorced from the direct experience of meditation, the Buddha's teaching can be misconstrued as nihilism. "Since everything, everywhere is impermanent," the argument might go, "and all my thoughts, feelings, and experiences are the illusions of my own parochial mind-and-body, and since there is no objective, external, solid place to stand, and everything I believe or know is only my own ignorant delusion, what is the point of anything? Cosmically speaking, what difference will my life make a million years from now? Why bother with all this effort to live the good life? Are the dinosaurs of the Triassic age benefiting from, or harmed, by their deeds? Let's live for pleasure now. There's no other realistic option. One hundred billion galaxies are not going to be bothered by what I do; not even the history of the earth is influenced by an ephemeral fire-fly like me. Nothing has any real importance. My philosophy is, *Whatever!*"

The Buddha's teaching, surveyed intellectually without personal experience, is also sometimes taken to justify contempt for mundane existence. "The goal of life is *nibbāna*, and that means all daily life and all social action is worthless. Our circumstances should be abandoned. We should withdraw into ourselves and seek our own salvation—after all, those were the Buddha's final words, and who are you to argue with Him? *Nibbāna* is entirely beyond the material world; therefore, disentangle yourself from the other ghosts around you and save yourself."

In fact, the impact of continuous touchdown on *anicca*, whether experienced while meditating intensely during a prolonged retreat or in a flash during daily life, is bidirectional. It both expands and focuses perspective. Life becomes bigger and more immediate. Touchdown on *anicca* holds together two implications: this moment is transitory, yet it is critical and formative.

The Buddha's teaching is that we are inextricably bound to every detail of our life. Through the operation of *kamma*, the cause and effect exerted by volition and action, we sculpt our fate across time, until we pierce through time itself into *nibbāna*. But the only avenue to that final release is a step by step, moment by moment pilgrimage along the path of compassionate interaction. The Buddha's last advice, to seek salvation within the island of ourselves, means that the Buddha himself is not a necessary condition to our release; we are sufficient to be our own masters. His final words did not mean, "turn your back on everyone else," which would be a contradiction of his forty-five years of working for the good of others in his own social and historical context.

Rather than nihilism or solipsism, the Buddha taught that every moment is creation of the future. We are all the fountainhead. Out of our awareness pours the next moment. Out of our era, the future gushes up. Out of our life steps the next one. There is nowhere to run.

It is true that vast infinitude stretches away before and after our brief visit to life. But it is also true that the past is being sieved through a fine mesh screen to make the material of the future, and we are that screen.

Meditation brings our attention to the micro-moment, which becomes drenched in hyperreality the way that tropical sunlight suddenly reveals the iridescence on the dove's neck. A play of pastel light brings every millimeter alive. The universe has no blind corners, no secret spaces. Every place, every moment, has the potentials of dark and light.

Salvation is not an elaborate cosmic project but a discrete engagement now. Every moment we are bowmen, shivering the future with the arrows of our thoughts and acts. In every irreplaceable interchange we mold the universe around us. The world is liquid, flowing, changing (*anicca*) and we are throwing touchdown passes that we ourselves will catch in the future.

VII

Is it really possible for an ordinary citizen to balance the nihilistic implications of cosmic time, with the obsessional, persnickety self-criticism implied by *kamma* and rebirth? Won't all students of the Buddha drift off into not-caring, or be clutched with worry that some misjudgment or bad-hair moment will have them reborn as rats in a Manhattan tenement?

Touchdown on *anicca* depolarizes thought; in fact, it punctures beyond thought, and balances reality just as it is, because *anicca* **is** just as it is. Touchdown on *anicca* kindles a balanced perspective that is intrinsic to the experience itself, as the next example shows.

A neurologist is seeing an elderly man whose family worries that he is deteriorating with Alzheimer's Dementia. To an outside observer—if there were one—of this medical evaluation, the doctor would appear factual, competent, medical, and unmoved. But inside of her, for all her white coat and reflex hammer and ophthalmoscope, is a fluttering thing. The neurologist herself has recently been suffering from severe medical symptoms that have as yet defied diagnosis by her doctors. She sees now in the patient in front of her a harbinger of her own looming decline. She thinks:

"What would happen if my mind began to slip, if I couldn't find words, got confused on facts? Would I be sued? Would my colleagues talk me out of practicing, or would I carry on until I harmed my patients? Will I die gradually, like this old fellow in front of me, fading like an October day; or will I be shot from within, a sudden thunderclap of stroke, pain, bewilderment, trapped in a contorted body and wordless?"

Fortunately, this neurologist is a Vipassana meditator, and as these countertransference fears rise up in her in response to her patient's plight, she finds herself automatically touching back down into the experience of *anicca*. She pauses for a moment, half listening to her patient describe how he got lost at night on the way from his bedroom to the hall bathroom, and she experiences the atomic world inside her, the physics of the stuff she calls herself, its dynamic, vibratory, active change in every second, its inevitable ultimate transformation by death, now, or tomorrow, or some day. The moment passes. She's back at work, but the covert pattern of her countertransference thoughts have changed subsequent to the experience of *anicca*.

"I can't control the future. I can't regulate or predict the time and manner of my death. But I can predict that death will come. The best preparation for it is not to philosophize about the meaning of life, but to turn every moment into an anvil on which I can forge a living, loving truth that is compatible with the reality of change, change, change. Someday, that will mean the courage to let go and dissolve totally beyond my current *self*, with confidence in the unseen future I will have formed. Right now it means, back to my patient." She says out loud:

"When did you first notice the decline in your ability to orient at night?"

VIII

The more deeply and the more often we touchdown on *anicca*, the more we realize both our insignificance, and our power. Vipassana meditation reveals *anicca*, the reality of incessant, pervasive, atomic change, within us. This revelation lifts a veil on both immediacy and transcendence. We are filled with the importance and the limits of life. Through Vipassana practice, this truth becomes readily available to us, as if we were each the pilot of our own private jet, and could negotiate any fog or storm to a smooth touchdown.

Karma and Chaos

by
Paul R. Fleischman, M.D.
and
Forrest D. Fleischman

I. Science and Karma

This essay addresses one difficulty that is encountered by meditators who have roots in the scientific tradition, and who may be troubled by an apparent clash between science and ancient Oriental descriptions of reality. The goal of the essay is to build an intellectual bridge between world views, over which a few students may walk towards meditation practice with less conflict or confusion. The following pages do not contain a complete description of either science or of the Buddha's teaching, but are intended to reveal passageways between the two through which a modern Western-based thinker can comfortably pass into a new world without feeling intellectually compromised.

The Buddha's teaching is built upon an understanding of the phenomenon of karma. *"Karma"* is a Sanskrit term that is often used in English, but for purposes of this essay I will use *"kamma,"* the same word from the ancient Pāli language which the Buddha actually used in his speech.

The twelve-fold chain of causality, which the Buddha said was the essence of his realization, is predicated upon the existence of rebirth. *Kamma* is the causal mechanism underlying rebirth. Although there have been Western apologists for the Buddha's teaching who have focused on his moral code and on his commitment to mindfulness in the current moment, and who have thereby tried to minimize the importance of *kamma* in the Buddha's dispensation, the

Buddha himself emphasized that the twelve-fold chain of causality, including rebirth, was the essence of his realization. He saw life as continuously and comprehensively lawful, a product of the ramification of action moving from life to life, across the barrier of death. Because all suffering is caused—often by deeds in past lives—it can also be eliminated when the cause is erased. Liberation from suffering, enlightenment, consists of understanding and acting upon the cause and effect relationship by which *kamma* leads to suffering or alleviates it.

To many Western students of meditation, *kamma*, with its implications for rebirth remains a fanciful and preposterous Orientalism to be disregarded. This attitude, however, alienates them from the heart of what the Buddha taught, and limits them to a surface understanding. Other Western students fully embrace *kamma* as the dogma of an orthodoxy in a self-gratifying, fairytale manner, that prevents the very inquiry into causality that the Buddha intended his teaching to evoke.

Kamma is a description of the origin of our personality—a unique conglomeration of forces, values, beliefs, predispositions, and reactions. These personality components were caused in the past, either within this life, or before, and they endure as ongoing traits. But they are not fixed. Through learning, effort, behavior and through insight based on meditation, the volition that underlies personality can change. Traditional Western psychology and *Kamma* are in agreement on this point. Classical Western personality theory certainly assigns a place to personality forces that antedate the environmental influences which begin to mold us at birth. These preexisting directives within personality are attributed to temperament and genetics. But the Buddha explained birth traits as deriving from choices and reactions in past lives. He built his future-oriented ethics on a version of causality continuing beyond this current life into a future life which will be molded by today's thoughts, reactions, and actions. So a student of the Buddha's teaching seems compelled to either accept *kamma* and reject scientific psychology, or vice versa.

When *kamma* is denied, the world is seen as a mixture of causality and fate. Causality operates now: the environment conditions us, and we make choices that express us—but genetics is mere fate. In this viewpoint, causes that lie outside of our own volition make us who we are. We are stuck with a hand that has been dealt by some other force. We are understood as subject to luck. Although we have some power to change, and although our current life follows the laws of cause and effect, our birth does not follow those laws. It is an irony that this world view, which is often mislabeled scientific, is based on a serial suspension of causality. The effects of our actions are believed to commence at birth and cease at death; before and after, personality submerges into a fatalistic, a-causal universe. In this description of causality, personality breaches out of the a-causal unknown, then exists and acts for sixty or eighty years, and then disappears again entirely, without further consequence.

Another feature of a world view which denies *kamma* is that ethics become local and diminished. No doubt there are moral ramifications of my behavior for me during my life, but not before or after, since there is no before or after. Ethics may well be important but of quaint proportion compared to the magnitude of fate that located me where and as I am.

To avoid these conundrums, some meditation students accept the idea of *kamma* as an opinion to be absorbed along with silence and observation. *Kamma* believed as dogma creates a magical world view devoid of examination, in which every turn on the road is attributed to a past life. Self-responsibility, rather than augmented, is eliminated. In this world view, a passive, acquiescent self-romanticization occurs. "This is happening to me because of my past life" becomes an unexamined, universally applied explanation that undercuts the search for right understanding and right action here and now. A description of reality that the Buddha intended to diminish ego is used instead to spin self-serving yarns. Dogmatic believers in *kamma* make up stories about themselves that have no threads strung to any reality beyond self-flattery. They impute causality to an invisible private fantasy of the past, and cease to examine this current moment as the node in which our future is embryonically alive and kicking.

How can a person who is fully committed to and culturally rooted in scientific thought make sense out of a meditation practice that requires neither rejection of, nor blind faith in *kamma*, but which deepens from insight into both the validity and the ethical ramifications of it?

In fact, this apparent dilemma is not a product of Western rationality and science at odds with Indian mysticism. Actually, this conflict stems from shallow stereotypes of science. As scientific thought has progressed, and as its models of reality have deepened in complexity, Western and Eastern world views have merged. The recent development of chaos theory in science is an example of this.

Chaos theory, which describes complex realities as viewed by contemporary science, is a window through which the scientific enquirer can see the world in a manner similar to the Buddha. It helps to elucidate many principles of *kamma*. It represents an advance from the oversimplified descriptions of cause and effect, which predominated in nineteenth and early twentieth century science. Chaos theory extends and replaces images of causality based on the mechanical, linear model, which until recently was considered the essence of science.

The mechanical model of reality explained aspects of the world whose operation is analogous to the interlocking cause and effect of gross, visible connections. The classical exemplification of the mechanical model in science was the behavior of billiard balls. For example, the angle and force with which a white ball strikes a black one can be used to accurately predict the subsequent velocity and direction of the black ball. Notice, however, that this form of science occurs within a fixed and artificial frame, symbolized by the walls of the pool table.

Since no one lives on a pool table, chaos theory is modern science's attempt to explain the total world we live in beyond fixed, artificial boundaries. It seems more applicable to natural phenomena like turbulence, weather, even personality. Chaos theory extends causal thinking into explanations more satisfying to the swirl of our existence than were the vectors of the artificial and limited world of billiards. The implication of chaos theory is that, in highly complex systems like the human being, causality operates in orchestrated, comprehensible ways that reveal coherence in the phenomenal world.

Previous scientific explanation, with its mechanical model of human life, posited a world of discontinuous causality. Death was viewed as a hiatus in the causal matrix of the world. It was as if the world were a lattice of events, each threaded to and pulling upon subsequent events, but the lattice had many ruptures, through which the new personality would crawl into life in this world, and through which it would ultimately dive out. This primitive, pseudo-scientific world view of the nineteenth and early twentieth century can be described as a theory of causality that is based upon discontinuous temporal and spacial segments of order, interspersed with randomness or caprice of the invisible. This is the world of the billiards game, where vectorial mathematics can predict the physical behavior of balls as long as they stay on the table but, if they go over the edge, they appear ruleless, bouncing around like crazy.

The Buddha taught, and chaos theory provides, another way to envision a world of unbroken causality without parenthesis or exception, based on an open-ended sense of time and space, and describing a world of variation and order governed by universal laws. This is the world of clouds and thoughts. An intellectual excursion through the world of chaos theory may provide some Western meditation students an intriguing tool to facilitate further depth in their practice. Of course, it should be kept in mind that chaos theory is a scientific enterprise and not a spiritual path to *nibbāna*.

II. Chaos

For hundreds of years scientists believed that the universe could be described by simple mathematical laws. Newtonian physics, for example, attempted to describe a clear mathematical formula to predict the relationship between orbiting bodies in the solar system.

Newton's mathematical model accurately described and predicted the motion of two bodies orbiting each other. But when a third body was introduced the computation became impossibly complex. While Newton's equations could describe the Earth orbiting the Sun, they became ineffective when applied to the Moon-orbiting-Earth-rotating-around-the-Sun. As the Moon rotates around the Earth, strong gravitational attraction of the Sun throws off its orbit. This in turn alters the Earth's orbit, because the Moon is pulling on the Earth, which, in turn again, alters the Moon's orbit. This process of continuous feedback—in which perturbations cause more aberrations which are then operative upon the original perturbations—cause the entire system to act chaotically. When the motion of a third body was included there was no periodicity, no easily describable structure. Even worse, the equation that could model the orbits of the entire solar system would have to take into account nine planets, fifty or so moons and uncountable asteroids and comets.

Newtonian physicists, unable to resolve this problem, decided that the effects of the other orbiting bodies must be small enough to allow them to be ignored. In the long run, they assumed, the Moon orbiting the Earth in the Sun's gravitational field could be assumed to be close enough to the behavior of the Moon orbiting Earth as if the Sun's gravitational field was not present. In order to explain and predict some events with mathematical precision, they had to ignore other events. They found it impossible to discover simple general laws to describe the complex patterns of nature. This type of simplification became standard among scientists; approximations would have to be good enough.

The models for three orbiting bodies were so difficult to solve because they involved a type of equation called a *nonlinear differential equation*. These equations are very complex. In each successive step of calculating, an operation is performed on the outcome of the previous step. But unlike linear differential equations, the value at the end of one particular step will not predict the value that the equation will produce ten steps down the road. Variation amplifies variation in unpredictable directions and with chaotic outcomes. In dealing with these problems, the pioneers of calculus focused on finding ways to *approximate* the answers of nonlinear equations. When data from an experiment showed nonlinear change, the scientists generally discarded the data, or blamed it on experimental error and found an approximate linear equation to describe the data. If this equation did not predict results accurately, the variance could be blamed on undescribable outside disturbances. Nonlinear equations became a backwater of calculus. Problems such as turbulence in fluids, describable only with nonlinear equations, were ignored.

With the advent of computers, in the 1950s, all this began to change. Computers could numerically calculate solutions to problems that would take lifetimes to solve by hand. One of the first people to apply computerized analysis to a nonlinear equation was a meteorologist named Edward Lorenz, who discovered three nonlinear equations which he believed would describe the core phenomena of what had previously appeared random and incomprehensible, i.e., weather. Lorenz posited that by studying the behavior of a relatively simple three-tiered system, he could gain insight into the complex atmosphere of the earth.

When he put his equations into a computer and graphed the results he found that, although vastly simplified compared to the many factors in the weather systems of the planet, the three equations produced startlingly variable behavior. The resulting variations expanded in many directions as the nonlinear differential equations were run through the computer. Three nonlinear equations, three statements, can produce a beehive of outcomes.

By changing the initial value in the equation by a tiny amount, say a ten-thousandth, he could drastically affect the value farther down the line. His three graphs initially seemed similar, almost identical, but after many iterations, they would diverge until they were completely different. To his surprise, Lorenz had generated behavior as unpredictable as weather from three fairly simple equations. He soon discovered that this was characteristic of all nonlinear equations. Instead of eliminating small differences, the equations magnified the differences, completely changing the outcomes of the graphs they produced.

The most commonly cited example of this magnification came to be known as the *butterfly effect*, which postulates that a butterfly flapping its wings in China today could cause a hurricane in Florida next week—the butterfly flutters the air in a tiny, unique way creating a subtle local heat gradient that builds up gradually over vast, oceanic open space into a stronger wind, which creates a high pressure system that moves across the Pacific, pushing moist air across Central America into the Caribbean. Based on Lorenz's research, contemporary meteorologists believe that if the state of the weather were measured over every foot of the entire earth, the information could not reliably predict weather conditions more than a couple of days in advance—the tiniest, undetected variation would magnify to completely change the weather within a few days.

Further analysis showed that similar patterns hold true for many systems. The economy, for example, has traditionally been thought to be a system in which prediction of future outcomes is possible if enough is known about present conditions. Classical economic theory describes a linear world. But students of nonlinearity have demonstrated that the economy is inherently unpredictable. Small changes can be greatly magnified in unexpected ways, whereas seeming macro-economic shifts may make little or no difference in long-term economic outcomes, depending on many contributing forces within the economy. Similar effects can be found in ecology, chemistry, physics, and even computer science. In the solar system example discussed earlier, it is possible that one of the small effects of gravity, say that of Pluto on the Earth's moon, could eventually cause the Moon's orbit to change drastically—perhaps allowing it to escape the solar system entirely.

Like the straw that breaks the camel's back, there is a certain level at which changes are more likely to have a drastic effect—to push the system over the brink, and into another state of being. The physical world contains zones of rules, called *attractors*. When a phenomenon moves towards the extreme edge of a zone, the attraction of a new zone, with new rules, may take over, altering the appearance and behavior of the original phenomenon.

This was another characteristic of nonlinear differential equations which Lorenz discovered. The data from his computer-generated graphs at first seemed to have no pattern. But after several runs, he observed that they were not actually anarchic even though they formed a strange shape. While the system never repeated and was not reliably periodic, it stayed within a defined range of values. This range of values, called the *Lorenz attractor*, shows a structure similar to that formed by many seemingly chaotic systems. Over a short time, the system appears patternless, but over a longer time, it maintains a general pattern. The weather on earth exhibits this same behavior. It does not suddenly turn into a frigid, vacuum state, nor does it reach temperatures at which atomic fusion can occur. It tends to stay within the range of -60 to 45 degrees Celsius. This temperature zone is the

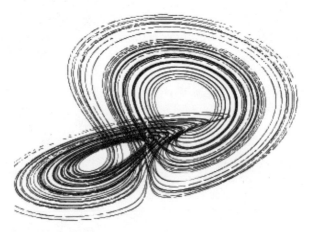

Graph of a Lorenz attractor

region to which the earth's atmosphere is attracted. In this region, there is an island of relative stability.

But if a system is sufficiently disturbed, it may jump into a very different behavior, orbiting another attractor. The Lorenz attractor, which describes the earth's temperature zone, is only one example of what are called *strange attractors*. The term, "strange attractors," highlights their unaccountability. Why, for example, does the earth's temperature remain in the zone it does, and not 100 degrees warmer or 200 degrees cooler! Strange attractors appear in many systems. Many attractors consist of multiple areas which serve as attractors, and other areas which repel the system. In other words, in complex, apparently chaotic, highly variable systems of mathematical formulae or of natural phenomena, there may be buffers, containers, locales, or channels that produce partial or temporary order. Some meteorologists now believe that the colder temperatures that occur during ice ages are the result of another attractor than the one that is operative today. In computer models, scientists have found that while the climate may orbit one attractor for a long time, it may spontaneously jump to another state, and begin orbiting another attractor. This mixture of temporary, partial order, followed by sudden, dramatic shifts to new semi-order located around new nodes, is characteristic of nonlinear differential equations, weather, and other complex aspects of the world.

One simple and therefore widely studied nonlinear differential equation is the equation used to model animal population growth in a finite environment: Next year's population = birthrate(population now)(1-population now) $[p_{n+1}=rp_n(1-p_n)]$. When the birthrate is low, the population tends to settle into a certain population level. This level is

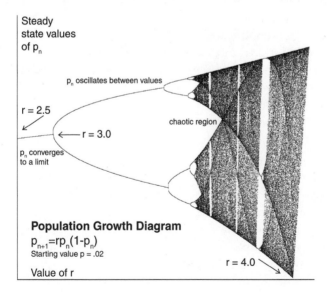

Steady state values of p_n

p_n oscillates between values

r = 2.5

r = 3.0

chaotic region

p_n converges to a limit

Population Growth Diagram
$p_{n+1}=rp_n(1-p_n)$
Starting value p = .02

r = 4.0

Value of r

an attractor. When the birthrate is higher, the population oscillates between two attractors. When the rate gets even higher, it begins to oscillate between 4, 8, 16 and 32 population attractors. At a certain point, when the birth-rate = 3.56999, the number of levels, or attractors, is infinite. The population seems to oscillate randomly. There is chaos. But, as the birthrate continues to rise, order appears again—the population begins to oscillate regularly again. Still, a slight change in birthrate is all that is needed to disrupt the oscillation. Even within the chaos, certain population levels seem to be attractors. Within the incredibly chaotic activity, there appears to be some level of organization.

As chaos became a legitimate field of study, a new type of mathematician appeared—one who experimented on computer in order to discover the behavior of nonlinear equations. Soon it was found that certain patterns hold true in chaotic systems no matter what differential equation was generating them. These patterns are newly discovered, universal mathematical laws, analogous to $2+2=4$. The implications are that no matter what equations are used, chaotic behavior will show some similar general principles. Even using simplifications of the equations needed to model the real world, the results seem to predict aspects of the reality that had once seemed lawless. Scientists, realizing that these systems could no longer truly be described as chaotic, called the emerging science, "complexity." Complexity is truly neither chaotic nor anarchic. Subtle attractors, repetitions and ratios direct even apparently wild events.

By the end of the 1970s, scientists were beginning to see the underlying order within the chaos of many real world systems and natural phenomena. They began to realize that the complexity of nature is not the result of a vast array of detailed instructions which dictate exact behavior for each and every situation. Instead, the complexity of nature is now understood to be the result of a smaller number of natural laws that permit both order and variety of possible outcomes. Like the rules of a baseball game, the scientific laws located within some natural systems set up a delineated, defined set of ordering principles and possibilities, yet, like the baseball game in action, numerous, almost uncountable results can occur within the context of the rules.

The science of complexity is the study of this mixture of imposition and variation within nature. There are now scientists whose specialty is the conceptual, mathematical or computer-based study of complexity—such as the collection of Nobel laureates and other distinguished scientists at the Santa Fe Institute in New Mexico. One of the hallmarks of complexity is that, at each new level of organization, new systematic behavior appears that is different than the sum of the behavior of the constituent parts.

An example of how new scientific laws emerge to govern phenomena at new levels of organization is the relationship of biology—life—to the constituent components of life-forms—atoms and molecules. The laws of biology are not merely extensions of physics and chemistry. Although our bodies are constructed of chemicals in their atomic nature—carbon, hydrogen, nitrogen, oxygen, etc.— you cannot brew up a person or an Irish setter by dumping the correct proportions of chemicals into a vat and mixing them together. Biological systems, living bodies, follow not only the laws of physics and chemistry, but their own living laws that emerge at the order of complexity we call "life." More complexity is not just an addition. More is different. New principles emerge within new layers of the world.

Furthermore, the principles within increased complexity are themselves governed by rules of efficiency or economy. The rule of order seems to be one of optimization. Substructures appear to organize themselves into more complex superstructures that are at lower energy levels, but this *most desirable* resting level usually appears only at what has been called *the edge of chaos*. The edge of chaos describes the mingling of fixed and fluid states during which optimal energy use and adaptation are most likely to occur.

Examples of the robust effect of the edge of chaos are found throughout biological and social systems. For example, if a system is rigidly ordered, then it will be unable to flex in response to external demands and environmental shifts, and it is prone to shatter. One thinks here of authoritarian governments, that impose dictatorial order for a brief period, but which crash when their leader dies or when outside stress becomes too great. On the other hand, a highly chaotic system tends to unravel into anarchy, in the way that, after the fall of Rome, Europe plunged into civil discord and cultural disarray. On the edge of chaos, a system contains enough order for self-perpetuation, and enough complexity to enable new combinations and permutations, new energies and new relationships to bubble up among the fixed corridors of precedent. One thinks here of the ideal democracy, whose laws hold at bay violence and anarchy, but whose discussions, dissents, and elections facilitate slow roiling of the political arena, to produce renewed governance of continuity and change. Fertile complexity endures longest at the edge of chaos.

Chaos theory is giving us a new window of understanding into how the world works. Instead of seeing the world as the result of many simple linear behaviors, we can now understand that the world is a manifestation of what may be a few, but very complex, nonlinear differential equations. The behavior of these equations are giving scientists great insight into the world that surrounds them. The discoveries that have been made in chaos theory are the scientific revolution of the late twentieth century, bringing the scientific world view one step closer to accurately modeling the complex universe in which we live.

III. Principles of *Kamma*

Kamma unites choice and necessity.

The concept of *kamma* has not fit easily into Western thought, since it expresses the unity of two elements: choice and necessity. *Kamma* is neither freedom nor determinism, as it has been often misread to be, but a dynamic fusion of these two, which in Western scientific thought were often considered opposites. But today, chaos theory points us towards a world view in which these opposites can be scientifically understood to act in concert.

The term *chaos* is a wry or paradoxical title for the new science, since its fundamental principle is that the wildest disarray is likely to contain some subtle coherence and order. At every depth, in every outback and attic, the universe is always a marriage between freedom and limits. The universe is neither as mechanical as a clock, nor is it ever totally a formless mist.

According to classical, linear science, the universe was construed as either lawful, or random, in different arenas, at different times. These two existed in polarity or divorce. If a phenomenon was lawful, then its underlying equations were thought to rule absolutely. If no exact law governed a realm of nature, then it was considered to be random. But in chaos theory, we envision degrees of order and disorder coexisting at the same moment at the same place. This coexisting complexity derives from atomic science, which construes the world as composed of loose particles floating among stationary columns and arches which are themselves composed of animated but compressed particles, and both the diffused and the solid can exchange constituents. Determinacy and non-determinacy, form and formlessness, mingle and cohabit in varying degrees at varying times and places. Lawfulness and randomness are degrees of each other. They are not in antithesis, but in fertile union. This atomic, complex synthesis of free choice and lawful consequence applies not only to the world of physics and chemistry, but to our psyches as well.

In each moment, our personal life also contains this union of choice and necessity. Though we often feel buffeted by capricious forces, disarray is illusory, and within even the storm is a downdraft of coherence.

Not every event that happens to us can be reduced to the direct linear consequence of a proximal antecedent. Storms of ancient origins may gust around us, and vast social maelstroms may sweep us up into historical events beyond our doorstep. But within even a hurricane, which appears to be pure chaos, lie the lines of scientific equations, and every hurricane eventually dies and reintegrates with the vaster body of nature, its rain once again resting in the ocean and its winds resorbed into the atmosphere. Similarly, people caught up in inscrutable events may journey along forcefields of love and compassion even within their vertiginous occasion.

By looking through the lens of chaos theory, we can see how *kamma* operates: our choices remain our own within the context of the unhinged and multifarious events of the world, and each of our choices will instantly begin to travel down the lines of cause and effect. Within the flux of the world we act, and the magnets of *kamma* draw out the implications. There exists indeterminacy, choice, but our actions organize the preexisting disarray into magnetic fields of effects. All moments and spaces of freedom are contiguous with vectors of consequence. Just as the hurricane always eventually resolves into ocean and air, everything we do is reintegrated with the electromagnetic tensions that our actions set into motion. If nature is the realm of the storm, it is also the zone of the magnetic field.

Chaos theory tells us the same thing when it describes its reality-modeling, nonlinear equations as being capable of both variable yet solvable outcomes. There is a *give*, a flexibility, in the world, which philosophers and theologians call *free will*, and which scientists designate as *chaos* or as loci of indeterminacy. We cannot predict the exact outcome of our own or anyone else's actions this afternoon. Each action bends meridians within a force-field of complex antecedents and impingements. Our actions occur in a dynamic world that resembles an endless billiard table with hundreds of balls upon it *already* whizzing along its surface in multiple directions. The fate of our ball partly hinges upon its own force and direction, but partly will result from other spheroids with which it may collide. We live in a stew of interactions. The impact of our lives occurs within a dense matrix of other lives, a historical moment with unique and oscillating concurrent companions with their own actions, interactions, and vectors.

But chaos theory reminds us that complexity is a far cry from anarchy. We may ricochet, but we can also steer. We may collide, but we may also resume our direction as often as we are bumped off of course. While we can't predict the outcome of one afternoon's choices and actions, we can become increasingly foresighted about the outcomes of continuous, recurrent, enduring efforts of direction, despite the interference of lateral collision or torque. Nonlinear equations and the laws of *kamma* describe enormous variability but lawful and coherent processes. Nonlinear equations and the laws of *kamma* remind us that within the sting of a hailstorm world, we can walk the path.

It is because the world is not capricious that true freedom exists. Our life direction is a product of renewed and recurrent momentum. Freedom is the presence, not the absence, of constraints that give ongoing impact and importance to our choices. Even skidding on the ice, we are behind the wheel. If we don't panic, and if we brake intermittently and steer into the skid, we can regain control of our direction.

The infinitely complex universe responds to an insistent whisper. We are sailing on ancient wisdom older than any one storm. *Kamma* means that every moment is connected to a past and a future and in that moment the material universe incorporates the pulses of love or hate, joy or dread, into its complex and multidimensional formulas.

In a little-known letter, Ralph Waldo Emerson described how the longer he lived, the more he experienced the power of fate, preexisting conditions, historical upheavals, accidents of birth, illness, war, oppressing the individual. Life seemed to be emphasizing the enormity of fate, the insignificance of the individual. He analogized his, and every person's plight, as living surrounded by conditions like a thick-walled cave of rock. Then he added that in one moment of *insight*, human consciousness could discover that the walls in every direction were fluctuant and soft, and could be molded by the pressure of human hands to assume new, airier shapes. Insight could melt the rocks of destiny. And when the moment of insight passed, the cave once again felt solid, but of new, personally sculpted dimensions.

Every locus of reality simultaneously vibrates with the ricochet of freedom, and rests upon containing antecedents and implications. The mathematics of the universe can simultaneously dictate and permit. Determinism and free will—the ancient antagonists of philosophy—can derive from the same nonlinear equations, which can both shape and contain phenomena without immobilizing them or reducing their internal variety to predictability.

In an infinite series of pulsatile moments, linearity and fluidity, determinism and free will, couple and uncouple, coexist. Those old philosophical dichotomies were based on illusions of unidimensionality and solidity. In fact the world is incandescent and infinitesimal. We exist between the moments. We shape not one but ongoing lifetimes of caves.

The implication of a proper understanding of *kamma* is to kindle a mood. Unlike the fatalism of the determinist, or the self-absorption of the existentialist, *kamma* properly understood simultaneously ignites acceptance and optimism. We accept our plight as our responsibility, and we seek fresh responses and solutions. Each moment we are the implications of our antecedent insights, and this is where we have come to be. And, each moment may be a doorway into a responsive and malleable new day.

Anatta, no permanent self.

Chaos theory provides models for understanding the Buddha's teaching of *anatta,* no permanent self.

The new science takes a leap beyond the theological assumptions that lingered within the world view of nineteenth and early twentieth century science. Then, causality was studied as it operated proximately in one basin of time and space. This echoed ancient theologies that focused on planet earth as the center of creation, and that described the world as being thousands of years post-creation.

But in chaos theory, and in reality as described by the Buddha, there is no point locus of creation, there is unending time and space, and the universe is uniform in nature, not geocentric. While the older sciences clung to their pool table universe—with solid feet on earth rock and with sharply delimited space—chaos theory carries us into a causal universe with no origin, no end, ongoing confluence and ongoing influence. There are no solid walls or absolute boundaries anywhere, and waves of effects pulse out from our actions to roll outward through time and space. We become citizens of expanse, continuity, and communication.

There are no impregnable islands in the universe, no true fortresses. There are no bounded spaces free of influences of other arenas. A false clarity emerges from studying the physics of billiard balls, without studying the motives of the man who holds the cue and strikes them. The more expansive the continuities we examine, the greater the complexity in outcome, the clearer the guiding laws, and the closer to universal truth we plumb. At the edge of every phenomenon are contiguous phenomena influencing it, the way that the orbit of the moon influences the orbit of the earth which influences the orbit of the moon—not to mention Pluto. Chaos theory derived partly from eliminating arbitrary constraints on the complexity of causal interactions. Accurate explanations are not based on arbitrarily bounded time and space.

As with the universe and the pool table, there is no unique and final boundary around me. The forces that mold me, the choices made within those limits, keep on operating until extinguished, and they operate before and after what I, in ignorance or arrogance, arbitrarily designate as *me*. This skin of self is a temporary membrane in a universe of permeability. This one body/mind is neither the origin nor the end of what it manifests.

When wild grapes ripen in Massachusetts in September, and dry on their vines in the sun, they create locales of heady, pungent aroma. I have noticed on my runs past them that the smell hovers in a discrete locale—I am running, smelling nothing; suddenly I am passing through a thick river of grape tang, and equally suddenly I am beyond it, as if it had been wrapped in a skin of atmosphere. By mid-October, this divine guest has disbursed. This is the nature of our "selves," too.

The Buddha described *anatta*, no enduring self. There is no unique or final boundary around me. I am a transient and local expression of a combination of laws and choices, in a seamless universe whose equation I express. I am similar to an autumnal mist of grape.

Any description that rests upon constrictions to time and space reveals only the limits of the describer behind the description. There are many edges, many grape skins, but no finalities among the world of things. Fluid change is the nature of all bodies, worlds, and truthful equations. This earth, this universe, is one temporary shape of space within vaster cycles of order and change.

Unique Outcomes from Similar Action

Chaos theory clarifies why variable outcomes may follow apparently similar actions.

The main objection to *kamma* from the standpoint of linear thought is what can be called: *the skeptical critique.* Two people apparently pursue the same path, but get very different effects. "He and I both meditated in the same way for the same number of years, yet he ended up so different from the way I did. Surely, this disproves that the same cause always produces the same effect." There are five mistakes contained in this argument against the law of *kamma*.

In the Buddha's descriptions of reality, there is no enduring, permanent self hidden within us, but we do have individuality. We each have our unique history and personal constellation. People have different antecedents. While they toe the same starting line, one runner has bagel brunch in his stomach, while the other is empty in the gut. We all contain an enormously complex historical, social, psychological mixture of already existing, continuously operating past causes. We never in fact toe the same line as anyone else. We are riding through time astraddle different vectors that only briefly and occasionally parallel anyone else's. We are riding in the same train compartment side by side, but are on different lifelong journeys which parallel each other only today. This is the mistake of confounding proximity with similarity.

Secondly, when we measure effects, we do so at one or several points in time. However, the true impact of any action may endure beyond the time period of our measurement. Simple equations are solved, and settle into a final form of fixed numbers. But nonlinear differential equations, whose behavior more closely simulates reality, unravel continuously. Think of the difference between a person with a pencil doing algebra, versus Edward Lorenz's computer graphing numerous iterations of nonlinear equations. In terms of peoples' lives, this means that, when we look over at someone else and say, "He got this good result while I didn't," or "She got such a miserable outcome from which I was miraculously spared," we are confusing a temporary station with a conclusive and final outcome today, without remembering that tomorrow there will be more iterations of the equation. Let us see who will be king or beggar tomorrow, or the day after, or the year after that. We may be suffering, or benefitting, from any event, long after we have consciously remembered it. Even Freud emphasized that we suffer most from forgotten memories. The uniqueness of every person, plant and animal is forged over eons. Ultimately, time is on our side. Don't reach conclusions before you have run the whole experiment.

The third error in the argument versus *kamma* comes from the existence of force-fields, strong attractors, that may draw one seeker to truth and another to security, that may hold one person down on one plane while his neighbor ascends. Every meditator has noticed in his or her mind, strong attractors, where the mind seems powerfully drawn, and rotates in ignorance, like an ox seeking a bag of grain suspended out in front of its nose and so it trudges onward in a circle that powers the mill. How can we ever imagine that our meditation resembles anyone else's? We are all rotating to a greater or lesser extent in delusions we have long been chasing. Some particularly powerful force field may hold us . . . or release us. Nonlinear equations may spew forth results tightly belted within a particular zone for numerous iterations, and then suddenly spring free of that band of outcomes. We may have a long time to carry one weight from which our companions have sprung free.

A fourth error in the skeptical critique of *kamma* comes from neglecting the emergence of new laws at new levels of systemic organization. Nonlinear equations do not resemble arithmetic addition, and complex systems change in character, not just in quantity, as their complexity increases, in the way that biological life differs from chemistry sets. *More is different.* Not every component weighs the same in the final analysis.

The same event may emit different influences depending on what floor of the building it occurs, whether it is in the executive suite or the basement. You and I may think and act the same, yet find our paths diverging, because we are operating in different realms, under the influence of different laws, in the same way that different regions of the same nonlinear equation may behave differently. We have both planted lettuce seeds, but in what county, on what soil, in what season, and with what skill at tending our nascent crop?

The fact that systems are governed by new laws at different levels of organization also explains why *kammas*, mental or material actions, may differentially influence a life depending upon where and when they occur. Life in a meditation center may catalyze personality changes which would have been less easily obtainable elsewhere. We can say that the atmosphere or ambience augments events, or we can say that complex impinging variables shift the rules under which consequences unravel. *Kammas* are contextual. The truth is universal, but there are holy grounds and helpful companions who can ease our ascent.

A fifth error in the skeptical critique of *kamma* has to do with the butterfly effect, by which tiny differences can be magnified by time, space, and impinging variables, into huge effects.

One moment of clarity can change a life. We occasionally hear how sobriety comes to the drinker, or revelation to the cynic, in a flash.

A second of clear and objective mindfulness of sensations by a meditator can reverse powerful delusions, the way that a small flag waved by a brakeman can halt the advance of a powerful locomotive. Insight into our past ignorance flashes out of momentary realization of the impermanence of our self. A straw can break a camel's back; a minute perturbation may shift the orbit of a giant planet; one act of rage can alter your life forever; one second of impersonal self-observation can release a storehouse of ignorance.

The butterfly effect also has implications for the power of thought. The Buddha differed from his contemporaries, and from many modern ethicists, because he emphasized

the importance of thoughts *as* actions. He did not accept
the existence of thought as merely private and irrelevant.
Instead, he stressed mental *kamma* as the epicenter of volitions. Through the subtle butterfly wings of our fleeting
thoughts, great changes may be heralded in our world. Of
course, this doesn't mean that every thought has equal
power. Many may well be lines drawn in the water, erased as
they are etched. But other thoughts may enter into the sur-
rounding complexity of personality and over time amplify
into major patterns.

The implications of the butterfly effect for the skeptical critique is that, when two apparently similar people live
apparently similar lives, yet end up vastly different, they may
have been influenced by subtle, difficult-to-observe, yet
powerful thoughts and actions.

Meditation students sometimes ask, "How can a few
moments of purity and wisdom while I am meditating, reverse the patterns of my lifetimes, which have not only
shaped years of actions, but which have also shaped long
daydreams of mine about passion or retaliation even as I sit
here and try to meditate?" Moments of objective reality,
immersion in the experience of impersonal, ceaseless change,
may exert a long-term, life-transforming effect, the way
minute perturbations of local weather may influence the
climate of ecosystems. Revelation of the truth of impermanence may cancel the pull of a strong attractor.

Once I heard a learned Buddhist monk object to Vipassana meditation as a path of liberation, based on his accurate
observation that, since we all have millions of negative, ego-
centric reactions, it would take us millions of years of
meditation to release each one of them. He put his hope on
ascetic monasticism alone. His flawed argument shows the
importance of non-summative math, of the existence of
strong attractors, and of various equilibria existing within
the same causal context. In the mind of this monk, each of
our reactions has to be released one by one through

Vipassana, an endless task, made even more hopeless by the fact that we can actually generate reactions as we meditate. What this ascetic failed to understand is that, through the power of insight into ceaseless impersonal change—as is the proper focus of Vipassana meditation—we can, in a moment, release heaps of reactions and orbit in a new equilibrium around a new personal center. This isn't the expression of a shortcut, but of winter or summer in the same city, quiescence or eruption in the same volcano, hate or love in the same mind. Through meditation, we can not only be improved, we can be transformed, and this can happen in any one moment, and in many moments of many transformations. Just as a nonlinear equation can suddenly be triggered to a new equilibrium, our lives can be not merely improved, but reorganized around new motives, goals, and insights.

The butterfly effect not only accounts for variable outcome in lifestyle, but it implies that optimism is realism. Subtle, ephemeral realizations can transform your horizons. *Kamma* is not the product of arithmetic addition. Not all moments and actions have equal power. One brush with ultimate truth, may give you wings to fly over old storms. A moment of clarity may dissolve years of delusion. Any moment may bring a quality of liberation that doesn't merely subtract past ignorance, but that catapults your equation around a new and salubrious strong attractor called *a love of the truth and a conscious, compassionate life.*

Any moment of proper meditation may be your last rotation around anger and your first orbit in new mental worlds. Getting established in a new way of life, *entering the stream* may be your final strong attractor.

A Middle Path of Discipline and Receptivity

Chaos theory instructs us to look for the greatest adaptability at the edge of chaos. This is based on both mathematical models, and on observations of the natural world. Too much variability—chaos—is unstable, non-self-perpetuating, a mess. This is the realm of bloody political revolutions in human societies, and of flooded rivers in nature. Change is wild, violent, unpredictable—from the human standpoint, we say *destructive*.

But too much order is the realm of dogma and fossils, systems that are too rigid to flex when new situations arise, and so die out. In human society, this is represented by authoritarianism, that imposes stability at the cost of variability, and that becomes brittle, eventually breaking apart again into chaotic disarray. One thinks of feudalism or Soviet Bolshevism. In nature, overly ordered systems are typified by monocultures, where one plant dominates the ecosystem, until climatic change occurs, and, without alternative botanical strategies in place, the entire system disappears like giant ferns.

Chaos theory reminds us to look for optimal vigor and endurance where repetition and spontaneity mingle. When arenas of predictability rub shoulders with foment and upwelling, we find both continuity and creativity. One thinks of fertile soil covered by fresh seeds, or of the minds of studious teenagers, able to learn, and full of auroral ideas. To adapt to a changing world, we must have flexible stability, a varying yet centered response to events.

The Buddha's teaching intuitively placed his students on the middle ground, organized yet fluid. His teaching emphasized freedom from the codifications of organized religions and political institutions; but he also emphasized the necessity of continuous training. The Buddha's lifestyle, the Dhamma life, is a mixture of self-discipline based on morality and meditation, coupled to fresh apprehension of the reality of the moment. This is a middle path, combining devoted return to focus, and unbiased receptivity of the hubbub of the world. We can say that the Buddha taught his students to live at the edge of chaos.

The daily life of the devoted meditator is a life-zone where repetition intersects with uniqueness. Every day meditators anchor themselves in stillness and observation, and every moment the world is new, necessitating fresh encounters, decisions, and adaptations. The Dhamma life occurs at the intersection of character, discipline and immediacy. Sheltered in morality, concentration, and wisdom, the student of meditation sallies forth without preconception into the vibrating and polyseminous world.

This way of life differs from more unstructured and undisciplined, secular caprice, in which focalizing return to meditation is lacking, and daily life shifts towards the chaotic pole, with its narcissism, anxiety, familial decay, and rootlessness. The middle path at the edge of chaos also differs from inflexible, mechanical routines of religious orthodoxy and political tyranny, which suppress the daily apprehension of the rejuvenation of creation, with its opportunities and idiosyncrasies. Recent observations of complexity in nature have led to the maxim: the stablest systems include modulated instability.

During a meditation course, a student of the Buddha's way of life also encounters the psychological manifestations of the natural law that operates at the edge of chaos. Intensified order is brought to bear upon the mind; the hours are structured; behavior limited; concentration exponentially augmented, as the student limits his or her activity to stillness and meditation on sensations hour after hour. But then the well known irony of meditation reveals itself, as pure concentration triggers a roiling of benthic thoughts, dreams, visions and emotions that are stirred up from the realm of awareness of sensations. As order increases, so does mental fluidity and complexity, until the entire mind, conscious and unconscious is flowing on the surface. This is when students have fresh revelations, the creative, life-transforming realizations that meditation courses provoke—an example of the numinous potential of the psychological edge of chaos.

Meditation courses, and lifestyles built around the discipline of twice daily meditation, exemplify at the mental level the fertility of the edge of chaos. As routinization, order, and predictability of behaviors increase, the depths of the mind can more safely be permitted to surface. As people progress on the path over years, ancient flaws and errors can at last be acknowledged and let go; cherished visions can at last be given serious energy to unfold; repetitive patterns of thought and behavior can be surrendered as new options present themselves. Imagine a life recurrently focused on one core reality: the direct experience of change within the sensations that form body and mind. From this marriage to fluidity which Vipassana meditation creates, comes a life that is ironically more stable, directed, purposeful, while more deeply informed by the grottoes, caverns, and recesses of the psyche.

The most fertile oceans, like the Georges Bank, are located at the edge of the continental shelf, where it meets the depths. The Buddha's path, Dhamma, twinkles at the edge of chaos, where adherence to truth glides among fresh, multivalent, receptive moments.

Aggregation, Dissolution, and Reaggregation

It is remarkable to see certain nonlinear equations graphed on a modern graphing calculator, because unlike any graph of linear equations, this line may show a smooth array, but suddenly become so variable that it expands into an apparently random scatter-gram of dots, and then just as suddenly, the line may re-cohere—all of this unraveling from the same equation, which takes different forms in different regions of its own influence. The same impetus may lead to aggregation, dissolution, and reaggregation over time. The same mathematical law may underlie varying formations, which appear different in their local manifestations, but which express the same, single truth.

This graphic expression of nonlinear mathematical formulas is entirely different than the graphs of all other formulas which may take regular shapes—like parabolas or hyperbolas—or which may be irregular waves or lines, but which are continuous and connected. The implication of nonlinear equations is that one law can manifest in varying forms, which bear no superficial resemblance to each other, yet which express the same relations in different contexts. And this is not just a mere mathematical game, since these equations seem to mirror aspects of our world.

Scientists studying population, for example, have found that simple logic, linear thought, does not accurately portray population dynamics. One would expect that the population of an animal species would grow until limitations of food or space, or until disease or predation, leveled off population at the maximum sustainable carrying capacity. While this simple logic often seems true, at other times populations seem to vacillate high and low, or to change erratically, or to temporarily semi-stabilize in one oscillating zone, or to fluctuate wildly and randomly, only to be followed by predictability and stability again. These numerous outcomes can be predicted by just one nonlinear equation, which, simple as it is, travels through all these options, at times expressing itself as a line, at times branching into a dendritic filagree, at times pulverizing into dots and fragments, then amalgamating into a new line that continues the original outward growth.

This behavior of mathematical equations may also provide us a way of understanding the reappearance of previous life—rebirth—and the appearance of new worlds in the vast flux of space and time. We do not need a mystical fantasy to account for the fact that there are more worlds within heaven and earth than we have dreamt of in our philosophy. Math and science remind us that ancient forces may cross regions of pure flux, and once again reestablish their trajectory.

This may help us draw closer in thought to an understanding of rebirth.

From one equation, from one action, from one ordering force, outward flow lines delineated by the mathematical statement, or consequences from our actions. As these derivatives emerge over time, however, they do not always look the same. In fact, a casual observer, or an observer who has access only to one area of the graph, one moment in time, may see no pattern at all. At certain regions of expression, the very same originating equation or action produces manifestations that appear to be completely different from its own manifestation a moment ago. The wavy line suddenly becomes random fragments and dots. A moment further on in the course of time, however, and the mathematical expression of the original equation has once again become a wavy line.

In the same way, forces set in motion by volitions of the human heart may have a long and variously appearing trajectory, at times visibly coherent, and at times moving onward without visible or congealed form. As the strong forces, or *kammas*, continue in time, however, they once again emerge, bounded by the visible forms called bodies.

Many possibilities may arise from and express the original volition. While there is great variation, there is not, however, lawlessness. Just the opposite—the variation is limited and contained within the possibilities of the volition of the originating moment.

How extraordinary a human life becomes when we envision it as the multifaceted expression of nonlinear equations deriving from our volitions and actions, and our lives consisting of thousands or millions of such inceptions. We are a fountainhead of events, rumbling on across time, each one mingling variability with predictability, so that our time on earth becomes a medusa's head of equations of what we have done here. What powerful computer could graph the outcome of all these possibilities?

But not every graph will unravel forever. Of the forces inside our volitions, only a few will have the momentum to keep on rolling, and to display the scientific truth, as revealed in nonlinear equations, that they can reemerge after having dissolved earlier on.

Thus, out of our wild proliferation of wave-form-effects of our thoughts and actions into the world, a few will behave like powerful nonlinear equations and will cross time and space to reemerge in *new* coherent, embodied form.

Out of the even vaster array of events that we all produce in this world-era of time, will come the laws, the equations, the volitions and actions, that will persist beyond the temporary dissolution of the world.

And this world, today, is itself only one reemergence of other past worlds whose equations scattered and re-cohered into this current world.

It is scientifically compatible to envision our lives as products of unending causality from the past which continues to operate in the moment. It is scientifically compatible to envision our lives as causal nexus out of which future conditions will evolve. This evolutionary process did not begin with planet earth, but with the processes which led to earth; and the process does not terminate when I die or when the earth burns out. As we have already seen, the billiard-table image of science, with its spacial limitations and temporal finalities, is an archaism, which has been replaced by continuities which link any one time-space segment to all others. Within this infinitely interlocking, causally communicating universe, aggregation, dis-aggregation, and reaggregation are commonly recurring, linked phenomena. Aggregations, minds and bodies, are expressions of forces, laws, equations, that also may have molded past bodies, and which may crystallize future bodies. The science of chaos, and the mathematics of nonlinear equations, tell us that our bodies are scintillating conglomerates of particles that aggregated according to law, will dissolve according to law, and may or may not aggregate again, according to the laws we activate and set in motion.

Every moment we are traveling the path of our volitions in a densely woven and lawful universe. We are ourselves the mirrors and consequences of antecedents whose origins recede into the eternity that has preceded us. And today we are our own microwave towers, transmitting into the future the *Kammic* radiations of ourselves. There is no corner pocket on the billiard table of the universe to catch and arrest the momentum we have set in motion with our cue.

The world we see, contact, and believe in is not the limit of the world. There is formation and flux, known and unknown in everything around us. There are many horizons but no finalities. Beyond this horizon, if we travel that far, is another horizon. Beyond the edge of the world are other worlds that dwell within and beyond all other worlds. Yet none are sealed, none absolutely bounded, none solid, but all mingle order and chaos, what exists with what is coming to be. And each new moment echos from the causes of the past, exfoliates out of the previous moment, carries the momentum of the moment before.

Chaos theory helps us to understand the world as the Buddha described it, and provides a scientific model that elucidates the Buddha's world view, but does not go further than that. Contemplation of chaos theory cannot substitute for moral lifestyle and meditation practice, nor does it even hint at *nibbāna*, transcendence of mind and matter, freedom from suffering, which the Buddha extolled as the goal of the path, and which eludes any description of the material world, no matter how sophisticated. Chaos theory elucidates some aspects of Dhamma, but not others. To activate the path and obtain its fruits, we need to attune ourselves to *kamma* and subsume our lives to its hegemony. Our morality and meditation—not our mathematics— shapes our destiny. To the extent that conceptual thinking inspires right action, it is a useful component of right understanding.

That is why the way we live in this moment, among the corporations and the tough customers and the backaches and the family dissent and the entrance examinations, is genesis. We are creating our future and participating in the future of many worlds.

Every moment a brand new universe is born from the iterations of the same old universal laws.

We are effervescent, and our lives are messages to the future.

Let our equations be truth, our radiations be love and light, our *kamma* be the laws of peace and harmony that will keep flowing across faithfully transmitting universes.

About the Authors

Forrest D. Fleischman wrote the original draft of "Karma and Chaos" for a math class during his junior year at Amherst Regional High School. He now attends Stanford University.

Paul R. Fleischman, M.D., has practiced psychiatry for more than twenty-five years. The American Psychiatric Association awarded him the Oskar Pfister award in 1993 for his "important contributions to the humanistic and spiritual side of psychiatric issues" as presented in the book *The Healing Spirit* (Paragon House, New York, 1989). His most recent book is *Cultivating Inner Peace* (Tarcher/Putnam, New York, 1997). With his wife, Susan, he took his first Vipassana meditation course under the guidance of S.N. Goenka in India in 1974. In 1987 the Fleischmans were appointed assistant Vipassana teachers, and in 1998, Goenkaji named them teachers.

Contact Information for Vipassana Centers

Courses of Vipassana meditation in the tradition of Sayagyi U Ba Khin as taught by S.N. Goenka are held regularly in many countries around the world. Worldwide schedules, information and application forms are available from the Vipassana website: www.dhamma.org. *Information may also be obtained from the following primary centers:*

Australia

Vipassana Meditation Centre   *Dhamma Bhūmi*
P.O. Box 103, Blackheath, NSW 2785
☎ [61] (2)4787-7436; Fax: [61] (2) 47877-7 221
Email: info@bhumi.dhamma.org

Vipassana Centre Queensland   *Dhamma Rasmi*
P.O. Box 119, Rules Road, Pomona, Qld 4568
☎ [61] (7) 5485-2452; Fax: [61] (7) 5485-2907

Vipassana Meditation Tasmania   *Dhamma Pabhā*
GPO Box 6A, Hobart, Tas 7001
☎ [61] (3) 6263-6785
Email: mjr@southcom.com.au

France

European Vipassana Centre   *Dhamma Mahī*
"Le Bois Planté," 89350 Louesme, Champignelles
☎ [33] (386) 45-75-14; Fax: [33] (386) 45-76-20
Email: info@mahi.dhamma.org

Germany

Vipassana Meditationshaus   *Dhamma Geha*
Kirchenweg 2; 76332 Bad Herrenalb
Tel: [49](7083) 51169; Fax: [49](7083) 51328
Email: dhammageha@aol.com

India

Vipassana International Academy   *Dhamma Giri*
P.O. Box No. 6, Igatpuri 422 403 (Dist. Nasik), Maharashtra
☎ [91] (2553) 84076, 84086; Fax: [91] (2553) 84176

Vipassana International Meditation Centre   *Dhamma Khetta*
12.6km. Nagarjun Sagar Road, Kusum Nagar, Vanasthali
Puram
Hyderabad, 500 070 A.P.
☎ [91] (40)402- 0290, 402- 1746
    City off. [91] (40) 473-2569; Fax: [91] (40) 241-005
Email: bprabhat@hd1.vsnl.net.in

Vipassana Centre   *Dhamma Thali*
P.O. Box 208, Jaipur 302 001, Rajasthan
☎ [91] (141) 641-520

KutchVipassana Centre   *Dhamma Sindhu*
Gram Bada, Dist. Mandvi, Kutch 370 475, Gujarat
☎ [91](283) 420-076; Fax:[91](283) 420-997

Vipassana Centre   *Dhamma Gaṅgā*
Baro Temple, Sodpur, Panihati (Calcutta) 743 176, West Bengal
☎ [91] (33) 553-2855
City off.: 9 Bonfield Lane, Calcutta 700 001
☎ [91] (33) 251 767, 258 063; Fax: [91] (33) 275 174

Himachal Vipassana Centre   *Dhamma Sikhara*
above Elysium House, Macleod Ganj, Dharamsala 176 219
Dist. Kangra, H.P.
☎ [91](189) 221-309; Fax: [91](189) 221-578

Japan

Japan Vipassana Centre   *Dhamma Bhānu*
Aza-hatta, Mizuho-Cho, Funai-Gun, Kyoto-Fu 622-0324
☎ & Fax: [81] (771) 860- 765
Email: info@bhanu.dhamma.org

Myanmar

Vipassana Centre   *Dhamma Joti*
Nga Htat Gyi Pagoda Road, Bahan Township, Yangon
☎ [95] (01) 549-290; Fax: [95](01) 289-965

Nepal

Nepal Vipassana Centre   *Dharmashriṅga*
Budhanilkantha, Muhan Pokhari, Kathmandu
☎ [977] (1) 290 655, 290 669
City off.:Jyoti Bhawan, Kantipath, P.O. Box 133, Kathmandu
☎ [977](1) 225-490; Fax: [977] (1) 224-720, 223-6306

New Zealand
Vipassana Centre   *Dhamma Medinī*
   Burnside Road, RD3 Kaukapakapa
   ☎ [64] (9) 420-5319

Sri Lanka
Vipassana Meditation Centre   *Dhamma Kūṭa*
   Mowbray Galaha Road, Hindagala, Peradeniya
   c/o: Mr Brindley Ratwatte, 262 Katugastota Road, Kandy
   ☎ [94] (8) 34649; Fax: [94](01) 573-054

Thailand
Thailand Vipassana Centre   *Dhamma Kamala*
   200 Yoopasuk Road, Behind Thairath School
   7, Tambon Dongkheelek, Amphur Muang, Prachinbrui,
   For registration contact: c/o Mrs Pornphen Leenutaphong
   929 Rama I Road, Patumwan, Bangkok
   ☎ [66] (2) 216-4772; Fax: [66] (037) 403-515
   Email: pornphen@bkk.a-net.net.th

United Kingdom
Vipassana Centre   *Dhamma Dīpa*
   Harewood End, Hereford, HR2 8NG, England.
   ☎ [44] (1989) 730 234, Fax: [44] (1989) 730 450
   Email: info@dipa.dhamma.org

U. S. A.
Vipassana Meditation Center   *Dhamma Dharā*
   P.O. Box 24, Shelburne Falls, MA 01370
   ☎ [1] (413) 625-2160; Fax: [1] (413) 625 2170
   Email: info@dhara.dhamma.org
California Vipassana Center   *Dhamma Mahāvana*
   P.O. Box 1167, North Fork, CA 93643
   ☎ [1] (559) 877 4386, Fax: [1] (559) 877 4387
   Email: info@mahavana.dhamma.org
Northwest Vipassana Center   *Dhamma Kuñja*
   P.O. Box 345, Ethel, WA 98542
   ☎ [1] (360) 978-5434; Fax: [1] (360) 978-5433
   Email: info@kunja.dhamma.org
Southwest Vipassana Meditation Center *Dhamma Sirī*
   P.O. Box 190248, Dallas, TX 75219
   ☎ [1] (214) 521-5258, 932-7868; Fax: [1] (214) 522-5973
   Email: info@siri.dhamma.org